the food of
ITALY

the food of
ITALY

Photography by Chris L. Jones
Recipes by Sophie Braimbridge
and Jo Glynn

MURDOCH
BOOKS

CONTENTS

FOOD JOURNEYS IN ITALY

the food of
ITALY

THE BEAUTY OF ITALY'S FOOD IS IN ITS GASTRONOMIC
DIVERSITY. EACH AREA IS LOYAL TO ITS SPECIALITIES,
AND INGREDIENTS AND RECIPES CHANGE FROM THE
MOUNTAINS TO THE COAST, FROM THE SOUTH TO THE
NORTH, AND THE MAINLAND TO THE ISLANDS.

This regionality is historically attributed to the individualism of
the sovereign states that made up Italy until the nineteenth
century; to foreign influences; and to the geography that saw
rice and polenta grow in the North, wild boar find a home in
the forests of central Italy and tomatoes and aubergines
prosper in the sunbaked South.

Indeed, before the Second World War, Italy really could be
divided up geographically by its cuisine: the North ate butter,
polenta, risotto and stewed meats; the Centre cooked with
lard and fresh pasta; and the South lived on olive oil, dried
pasta, pizza, chilli pepper and tomatoes. In the past fifty
years, with the movement of people from the South to the
North and from the country to the city, this has changed.

Yet *cucina regionale* (regional food) is still very much alive.
Despite industrialization, the European Community and the
changing face of the countryside, the artisanal skills that are
the foundation for *cucina regionale* remain, and there is pride
in the production of local foods like cheeses, hams, oils and
pasta. Wine is also a regional speciality—at many restaurants,
the choice is simply between a carafe of local red or white.

Italy is also the home of the Slow Food Movement, which
champions the cause of regional food and tradition. Indeed,
the whole country is undergoing a nostalgia for regional
cooking and for *cucina povera* (the food of poorer southern
Italy). Even in restaurants that don't specialize in regional
food, dishes with traditional ingredients such as beans,
chestnuts, grains and wild salad leaves are very popular.

Through an arch of the Ponte delle Torre is seen rural Umbria, home to wild boar and truffles. This granite stall in Naples makes slushy ices, while a *gelateria* in Verona sells outstanding ice cream. Tuna is one of the prize catches in Sicily and bright peppers are used in the dishes of the South. A Campari sign lights up Palermo at night and by day men sit in the street to talk.

7

Italy's climate gives the produce intense flavour and colour: purple aubergines; red tomatoes; sweet cherries; meaty mushrooms and fat olives, crushed to tapenade. Food is found everywhere, from Bologna's markets to cafés in Naples' Galleria Umberto I and *salumeria* in the backstreets. A grenadine is served at Florian's in Venice and Torre Ghirlandina overlooks Modena's market.

8

Eating and drinking well is a national pastime — from selecting fresh vegetables in the market to having a mid-morning espresso in a café, lunching in a simple *trattoria* or *osteria,* and picking up some antipasto from the *salumeria* on the way home from work.

To many Italians, food shopping is practically a full-time job. Shops open twice a day so you can buy once for lunch and then again for dinner. Every city, town and village has at least one market, where the produce is more seasonal than that available in the supermarkets and standards are high as stalls compete for shoppers. Apart from the *alimentari* (general stores), there are a number of specialized food shops you would expect to find in every Italian town:

The *caseificio* and *latteria* sell dairy products and often eggs. These can be part of the dairy itself.
The *enoteca* sells wine, by the bottle and also often by volume from huge containers.
The *macelleria* (butcher) sells fresh meat and poultry.
The *norcineria* is named for the famed butchers of Norcia (*norcini*), and sells salumi (cured pork products).
The *salumeria* also sells salumi, along with prepared foods like fresh pasta and speciality items.
The *panificio, panetteria* and *forno* sell breads and baked goods. They bake twice a day, once for each opening.
The *pasticceria* sell pastries.
The *pescheria* is the fishmonger.
The *rosticceria* is a very upmarket take-away, selling spit-roast chickens, meat and other prepared foods.
The *frantoio* is an olive oil mill or a shop that sells olive oil. The oil can be bought by the tin, bottle or by volume like wine.
The *gelateria* is the ice cream shop, often doing a take-away trade in cartons, as well as cones and cups. Some have tables outside for serving more elaborate creations.

Italians love to buy at source and vineyards, cheese-, pasta- and salumi-makers often have shops where you can buy straight from the producer. Mozzarella can be purchased still warm from the dairy, pasta bought by the kilo at the factory, balsamic vinegar direct from the *acetaia* and fish off boats.

Cafés and bars are another mainstay of Italian life. In small towns they are the focus of the square and are usually occupied by a row of men drinking espresso or small shots from the bar. In and around Naples, your espresso may be sweetened by the *barista*, while in other areas it is up to you. Cappuccino is considered more to be breakfast than a drink and is never drunk after eleven in the morning.

THE FOOD OF THE NORTH

Encompassing Piemonte, Valle d'Aosta, Lombardia and Liguria in the northwest and Trentino-Alto Adige, Veneto and Friuli-Venezia Giulia in the northeast, the food of the North has been shaped by the influence of its northern neighbours and mountainous terrain. Polenta and rice are staples and its dairy products and wines are among Italy's best.

Piemonte is home to the highly prized white Alba truffle, sprinkled over melted fontina in Piemonte's fondue-like *fonduta,* over pasta or eggs. Delicious pastries are served in Turin's famous cafés, while Alba is famed for fine chocolate. This region also produces Italy's best grissini and some of its greatest wines, including Barolo and Barbaresco.

The mountainous Valle d'Aosta is most famous for its alpine cheeses, especially fontina, Toma and Robiola, which are central to the region's cuisine.

Lombardia includes some of the richest agricultural areas in Italy and has a very diverse cuisine. Many of Italy's finest cheeses, such as Gorgonzola, Taleggio, Bel Paese and grana padano are produced here, and fresh pasta, polenta and rice are all enjoyed, including the classic *risotto alla milanese*. To the north, Valtellina is famed for bresaola (air-dried beef) and pizzoccheri, a buckwheat pasta.

Ligurian cuisine is unusual in northern Italy for its use of basil, most notably in *pesto alla genovese*. This is eaten with *trenette*, tagliatelle-like noodles, gnocchi and in minestrone. The mountains behind the Riviera provide herbs for cooking, and specialities are focaccia and walnut sauce.

Trentino-Alto Adige can be gastronomically divided into two. Alto Adige to the north is Austrian Italy and the cuisine includes speck (cured ham), *canederli* (dumplings) and *gulasch*. Trentino is more Italian, though *canederli* are popular and the excellent apples of this region are made into a local strudel. Polenta and breads accompany meals.

Outside Venice, the food of Veneto is generally simple, from bean soups, such as *pasta e fagioli,* to risotto or *risi e bisi*. Venice is known for its unfussy preparation of seafood, such as *moleche* (soft-shelled crabs). Veneto is also one of Italy's great wine regions, making Bardolino, Valpolicella and Soave.

Friuli-Venezia Giulia, bordering Austria and Slovenia, is known for its *prosciutto di San Daniele*—an exquisite sweet ham.

People enjoy coffee or gelati on a Sunday afternoon in a Modena bar. Fresh produce is transported to the Rialto market in Venice by barge, then stacked up on stalls. Asparagus is a favourite addition to risottos in the North, while at Isola della Scala, Gabriele Ferron uses his own rice to cook up wonderful dishes like this salad. These famous amaretti are made in Lombardia.

11

Tuscany's hillls are covered with Chianti vines, while Siena's Duomo dominates a town famed for its panforte. The produce of Italy's centre includes cherries from Emilia-Romagna, figs eaten with the area's Parma ham, sweet peaches from Le Marche and tiny lentils from the hill-town of Castelluccio. Roast sucking pig (*porchetta*) is a speciality and Bologna's streets are full of restaurants.

THE FOOD OF THE CENTRE

The central region of Italy encompasses Emilia-Romagna, Le Marche, Tuscany and Umbria—some of the best-known gastronomic regions of Italy. This is an area of fresh pasta, great cheeses and salumi and robust wines.

Emilia-Romagna, stretching out west from the Adriatic, is renowned both inside and beyond Italy as the country's greatest region for food. Circling out from its centre, Bologna, the region produces some of Italy's best-known foods. *Prosciutto di Parma* is produced south of Parma and often served wafer-thin with bread, while the culatello, mortadella and *prosciutto cotto* of this area are all renowned. *Parmiggiano Reggiano* is eaten in chunks or grated over Emilia-Romagna's wonderful fresh egg pasta, which comes in more shapes and varieties than anywhere else in Italy and includes the region's favourite, tortellini. Fresh pasta is often served with Emilia-Romagna's ragù, reinterpreted worldwide as spaghetti Bolognese. *Aceto balsamico tradizionale di Modena* is an extraordinary vinegar, still made in limited quantities by ancient methods that produce an intensely concentrated flavour.

Le Marche is a self-sufficient area, separated from the rest of central Italy by the Apennines. It is renowned for its Adriatic seafood, used to produce local versions of the rich fish stew, *brodetto*. The local cuisine also makes use of its white and black truffles, wild mushrooms and fennel. Famed dishes include *porchetta* (roast suckling pig) and *vincisgrassi* (lasagne made with chicken livers and prosciutto).

Tuscan cooking is renowned as some of the simplest in Italy. The world's finest extra virgin olive oils are made here, served drizzled over Tuscany's unsalted bread. Meals are centred around meat, especially beef, soups such as *ribollita* and *papa al pomodoro,* and many bean dishes. Tuscans, in fact, are known as *i mangiafagioli*—the bean-eaters. Siena has its spicy cakes, *pan pepato* and *panforte*, that date back to medieval times, while Florence is famous for huge *bistecca alla fiorentina*. Tuscany's wines are exceptional, with Chianti being Italy's most famous red.

The only landlocked region in Italy, Umbria's food is hearty and simple. There are, however, some outstanding local products, especially the local truffles, wild mushrooms and great pecorino cheeses. Umbria is most famous for its use of pork—the town of Norcia gave its name to *norcineria,* meaning pork butcher—and its tiny lentils from Castelluccio.

THE FOOD OF THE SOUTH

Lazio, Abruzzo, Molise, Campania, Puglia, Basilicata, Calabria, Sicily and Sardinia make up Italy's South, home to robust *cucina povera* (peasant cooking) and a wonderful cuisine created from whatever was available: sun-ripened vegetables and fruit, wheat for dried pasta and local cheeses.

Surrounding Rome, Lazio is influenced by the unique food of its capital. Roman cuisine is not delicate and makes use of pasta, beans, artichokes, meat and offal. Its *spaghetti alla carbonara* and *bucatini all'amatriciana* both include the local *guanciale* (cured pig's cheek). In rural Lazio, lamb is used often in dishes like *abbacchio* (milk-fed baby lamb).

Abruzzo and Molise are mountainous areas with strong rural cooking traditions. Molise produces fine lentils, pasta and olive oils, while saffron is grown in Abruzzo, along with the *diavolilli* (tiny red chillies) that go into so many dishes.

The cuisine of Campania and Naples is famous throughout the world: spaghetti with tomatoes and basil, *spaghetti alle vongole*, pizza topped with fresh mozzarella and aubergine Parmigiana. As well as fresh mozzarella made from buffalo or cows' milk, there is good ricotta, goats' cheeses and caciocavallo. Lemons are used in granite and limoncello.

Puglia has had many foreign invaders, but the food remains quintessentially Italian. Orecchiette is a delicious ear-shaped pasta, served locally with *cime di rapa* (turnip greens) and good cheeses include caciocavallo, scamorza and pecorino.

Basilicata is one of the poorest regions of Italy, but its *cucina povera,* dominated by pasta and vegetables, can be delicious. Dishes and meats are spiced with *peperoncino*.

At the tip of Italy, Calabria has two coastlines, giving it plenty of seafood, particularly swordfish and tuna. Citrus fruit grow well here, as do figs and olives. *Peperoncino* adds fire to the cooking and there is excellent provolone and caciocavallo.

Sicilian food has long been influenced by invaders, particularly the Arabs who brought sugar. The island's *dolci* (sweets), granite and gelati are still considered Italy's best. There is also plentiful seafood, citrus fruit, and capers for making caponata. The Sardinians have traditionally looked more to their inhospitable interior for food than to their once mosquito-infested coast. The cuisine is based on sucking pig and lamb, pecorino, *pane carasu* (flat bread) and honey.

The flavours of the South: ripe tomatoes, citrus fruit, olives from twisted groves and fresh herbs. Palermo is home to both the Vucciria market, set in its backstreets, and a busy fish market, where the bellies of Sicily's famous tuna are cut out for export to Asia. Seafood is prepared simply, while marzipan fruit has been elevated to art. The grandeur of Naples is matched by its wonderful food.

15

ANTIPASTO, SALADS
& SOUPS

STUFFED MUSHROOMS

8 large flat mushrooms
1¹/₂ tablespoons lemon juice
12 button mushrooms
20 g butter
1 shallot, finely chopped
1 garlic clove, crushed
2 tablespoons white wine
100 g Parmesan, grated, plus
  1 tablespoon to serve
50 g fresh breadcrumbs
1 egg, lightly beaten
3 tablespoons double cream
1 tablespoon chopped tarragon
1 tablespoon chopped parsley

SERVES 4

PREHEAT the oven to 150°C (300°F/Gas 2). Wipe the large mushrooms with a damp cloth, remove and discard the stalks and rub the caps with a little lemon juice to keep them white. Wipe the button mushrooms and chop them finely, then mix with the remaining lemon juice.

HEAT the butter in a small frying pan, add the shallot and garlic and cook, stirring, for 4 minutes. Add the chopped mushroom and the wine and cook, stirring, for another 4 minutes. Remove from the heat and stir in the Parmesan, breadcrumbs, egg, cream and tarragon. Season.

PLACE the mushroom caps on a lightly oiled baking tray and stuff with the filling. Bake for 12 minutes. Sprinkle with the Parmesan and parsley and serve either warm or cold.

STUFFED MUSHROOMS

CHARGRILLED ASPARAGUS

24 asparagus spears
1 tablespoon extra virgin olive oil
2 tablespoons balsamic vinegar
Parmesan shavings

SERVES 4

WASH the asparagus and remove the woody ends (hold each spear at both ends and bend it gently—it will snap at its natural breaking point).

PUT the asparagus in a bowl, add the olive oil and toss well. Heat a griddle or barbecue and cook the asparagus for about 10 minutes, or until *al dente*. Drizzle with balsamic vinegar and sprinkle with the Parmesan to serve.

(IF YOU DON'T have a griddle or barbecue, you can steam the asparagus or boil in salted water for 6–8 minutes until *al dente*. Drain and mix with the olive oil, balsamic and Parmesan.)

CHARGRILLED ASPARAGUS

STUFFED PEPPERS

STUFFED VEGETABLES ARE OF ARABIAN ORIGIN, ALTHOUGH THEY HAVE NOW BECOME ALMOST SYNONYMOUS WITH MEDITERRANEAN COOKING. IN ITALY, YOU WILL FIND VEGETABLES STUFFED WITH ALL MANNER OF INGREDIENTS, FROM RICE AND BREADCRUMBS TO CHEESE OR MEAT.

3 red or yellow peppers
1 tablespoon olive oil
1 small onion, finely chopped
2 garlic cloves, crushed
50 g butter
175 g fresh breadcrumbs
1 egg
30 g Parmesan, grated
2 tomatoes, peeled, seeded and
    chopped
150 g mozzarella, grated
2 tablespoons chopped basil
3 tablespoons extra virgin olive oil

SERVES 6

PREHEAT the oven to 170°C (325°F/Gas 3). Cut the peppers in half and remove the seeds. Place on a lightly oiled baking tray.

HEAT the olive oil in a frying pan, add the onion and garlic and cook, stirring, for 5 minutes. Remove from the heat and stir in the butter and breadcrumbs. Transfer to a bowl and add the egg, Parmesan, tomato, mozzarella, basil and 3 tablespoons water. Stir well and season.

FILL the pepper halves with the stuffing, drizzle with the extra virgin olive oil and bake for 40–45 minutes, or until the peppers are cooked through and the tops are golden brown.

STUFFED ONIONS

8 medium white or red onions,
    peeled but left whole
3 tomatoes
1 tablespoon olive oil
15 g butter
1 onion, finely chopped
1 garlic clove, crushed
250 g minced beef
2 tablespoons chopped parsley
1 egg
4 tablespoons grated Parmesan

SERVES 4

PLACE the onions in a large saucepan, cover with water and simmer for 10 minutes. Drain and cool. Preheat the oven to 180°C (350°F/Gas 4). Score a cross in the top of each tomato. Plunge into boiling water for 20 seconds, then drain and peel. Chop the tomatoes, discarding the cores.

HEAT the olive oil and butter in a frying pan until the butter has melted. Add the onion and garlic and cook, stirring, for 5 minutes or until tender. Add the tomato and cook for a further 6 minutes over low heat. Add the beef and cook until lightly browned. Remove from the heat and cool. Add the parsley, egg and Parmesan and stir well.

CUT off the top of each onion and, using a melon baller or a spoon, remove some of the inside (being careful not to lose the shape of the onion). Place them on a baking tray and stuff with the filling. Bake for 20 minutes and serve hot or at room temperature.

ARTICHOKES VINAIGRETTE

ONLY SMALL YOUNG ARTICHOKES OF A FEW VARIETIES, SUCH AS VIOLETTO TOSCANO, ARE TENDER ENOUGH TO BE EATEN RAW. IF THEY ARE UNAVAILABLE, USE COOKED HEARTS, EITHER FRESH OR CANNED. ALLOW ONE HEART PER PERSON AS PART OF AN ANTIPASTO, TWO EACH AS A FIRST COURSE.

There are three different sizes of artichoke. The largest are the first to appear on the plant and are known as *la mamma* (the mother). Next to grow are the *figli* (children), which are smaller and more tender. Finally, the *nipoti* (nephews) appear further down the plant, the smallest and most tender of all.

2 tablespoons lemon juice
4 young Romanesco or Violetto
   Toscano artichokes
1 quantity vinaigrette (page 286)

SERVES 4

MIX the lemon juice in a large bowl with 1 litre cold water. Using kitchen scissors or a sharp knife, cut off and discard the top third of each artichoke. Discard the tough outer leaves and snip off any spikes from the remaining leaves. Chop off and discard all but 2–3 cm of the stem and peel this with a potato peeler.

SLICE EACH artichoke in half from top to bottom, including the stem. Scrape out the furry choke and discard it. As each artichoke is prepared, place it straight into the bowl of lemon water to avoid discolouring.

SHAKE EACH artichoke half dry and arrange on a serving platter. Spoon the vinaigrette over the top and leave for at least 30 minutes before serving.

WARM ARTICHOKES VINAIGRETTE

4 x 350 g artichokes
juice of 1 lemon
1 quantity vinaigrette (page 286)

SERVES 4

BRING a large pan of salted water to the boil. Cut off the artichoke stalks at the base so the artichokes stand upright. Put them in the boiling water and add the lemon juice. Boil gently for 30–40 minutes or until a leaf from the base comes away easily. Cool quickly under cold running water and drain upside down on a tray.

TO SERVE, put each artichoke on a serving plate and gently prise it open a little. Spoon the vinaigrette over the top, letting it drizzle into the artichoke and around the plate.

(TO eat the artichokes, scrape off the flesh from the leaves between your teeth, then remove and discard the furry choke at the base with a spoon. You can now eat the tender base or 'heart'.)

WARM ARTICHOKES
VINAIGRETTE

BRUSCHETTA

4 large slices of 'country-style'
  bread, such as ciabatta
1 garlic clove
drizzle of extra virgin olive oil

MAKES 4

GRILL, chargrill or toast the bread until it is crisp.
Cut the garlic clove in half and rub the cut edge
over both sides of each bread slice. Drizzle a little
olive oil over each bread slice.

TOMATO AND BASIL BRUSCHETTA

4 ripe tomatoes
1 tablespoon shredded basil
4 pieces basic bruschetta

SERVES 4

ROUGHLY chop the tomatoes and mix with the
basil. Season well and pile onto the bruschetta.

Bruschetta is a traditional Italian
antipasto. Use slightly stale
bread (this is an excellent dish for
using up leftovers) that is dense
enough to stop the olive oil
seeping through. Technically
speaking, real bruschetta is just
plain grilled bread, rubbed with
garlic while it is still hot and then
drizzled with good-quality olive oil.

WILD MUSHROOM BRUSCHETTA

2 tablespoons olive oil
400 g selection of wild mushrooms,
  particularly fresh porcini, sliced if
  large or chestnut mushrooms
2 garlic cloves, crushed
1 heaped tablespoon chopped
  thyme
4 pieces basic bruschetta

SERVES 4

HEAT the olive oil in a large saucepan or frying
pan. When the oil is hot, add just enough
mushrooms to cover the base of the pan and
cook over high heat, stirring frequently. Season
with salt and pepper. (Sometimes the mushrooms
can become watery when cooked. Continue
cooking until all the liquid has evaporated.)

ADD a little crushed garlic and thyme and cook
for a further minute. Remove from the pan and
repeat with the remaining mushrooms. Spoon
over the bruschetta and serve immediately.

AUBERGINE BRUSCHETTA

2 large aubergines, sliced
2 garlic cloves, crushed
150 ml extra virgin olive oil
juice of 1 small lemon
3 tablespoons roughly chopped mint
4 pieces basic bruschetta

SERVES 4

HEAT a griddle on the stove. Place a few
aubergine slices on the griddle and cook over
moderately high heat, turning once, until the
aubergine is soft and cooked.

MIX TOGETHER the garlic, oil, lemon juice and
mint and season well. Put the aubergine in a dish
with the marinade and leave for 30 minutes. Place
a couple of aubergine pieces on each bruschetta
and spoon the marinade over the top.

AUBERGINE BRUSCHETTA

DEEP-FRIED COURGETTE FLOWERS

THOSE WHO GROW COURGETTES AT HOME CAN MAKE USE OF THE YELLOW FLOWERS THAT APPEAR IN STEADY SUPPLY THROUGHOUT THE SUMMER. IF FLOWERS AREN'T AVAILABLE, YOU CAN USE THE SAME BATTER AND METHOD TO DEEP-FRY SLICES OF COURGETTE AND AUBERGINE.

BATTER
50 g plain flour
2 teaspoons olive oil
3 egg whites

8–12 courgette flowers
oil for deep-frying
lemon wedges

SERVES 4

TO MAKE the batter, sift the flour into a bowl and stir in 1/4 teaspoon salt. Mix in the oil with a wooden spoon, then slowly add 75–100 ml warm water, changing to a whisk when the mixture becomes liquid. Continue whisking until the batter is smooth and thick. Whisk the egg whites until stiff peaks form, then fold into the batter.

CHECK the courgette flowers are clean and aren't hiding any stray insects. Trim the stem of each flower to about 2 cm (this gives you something to hold on to when dipping).

HEAT the oil in a deep-fat fryer or deep frying pan to about 180°C (350°F), or until a piece of bread fries golden brown in 15 seconds when dropped in the oil. If the oil starts to smoke it is too hot.

DIP the courgette flowers into the batter, coating both sides. Fry the flowers in batches until golden brown, turning once to cook on both sides. Drain on paper towels and serve with a sprinkling of salt and a lemon wedge. Don't let them sit around— serve and eat immediately, preferably with a glass of chilled white wine.

Courgette flowers can have a baby courgette attached, while others are simply the male flowers of the plant and have a long stem instead of a courgette. Choose flowers that are fresh and firm.

CIPOLLINE AGRODOLCE

1 kg small onions (cipolline or
   pickling onions)
2 tablespoons brown sugar
2 tablespoons white wine vinegar
60 g butter

SERVES 8

PEEL the onions, cut off the roots and remove the first layer of skin. Heat the sugar in a large heavy-based saucepan until it melts and starts to caramelize. Remove from the heat, add the vinegar and butter and stir well. Return to the heat, bring to the boil and add the onions. Add enough water to just cover the onions and simmer for 10 minutes. Cover the saucepan and simmer for another 20 minutes, or until the onions are tender. Serve hot or at room temperature.

CIPOLLINE AGRODOLCE

CROSTINI

2 day-old ciabatta or 1 day-old
  pugliese
200 ml extra virgin olive oil

MAKES 50

TO MAKE the crostini, preheat the oven to 180°C (350°F/Gas 4). Thinly slice the bread, cut each piece into quarters and drizzle olive oil over both sides. Lightly toast in the oven until just crisp. The crostini will keep in an airtight container for at least a couple of days.

TAPENADE CROSTINI

250 g whole black olives, pitted
50 g tin anchovy fillets
1 tablespoon capers, drained
2 garlic cloves, crushed
15 g basil, finely chopped
grated zest and juice of 1 lemon
200 ml extra virgin olive oil

FINELY CHOP the olives, anchovies and capers together with a knife or food processor and place in a bowl. Add the garlic, basil, lemon zest and juice, stir in the olive oil and season well.

SPREAD on crostini to serve. (The tapenade will keep in an airtight container in the fridge for up to a month.)

Crostini are best made from slightly stale leftover bread and topped with pâté, ragù or vegetables. This is an antipasto that is particularly associated with Tuscany.

RED PEPPER CROSTINI

3 tablespoons olive oil
1 onion, finely chopped
2 red peppers, thinly sliced
2 garlic cloves, crushed
1 tablespoon capers, drained and
  chopped
2 tablespoons balsamic vinegar
1 tablespoon roughly chopped flat-
  leaf parsley

HEAT the olive oil in a frying pan and cook the onion for a few minutes until soft. Add the peppers and cook for a further 15 minutes, stirring frequently. Season. Add the garlic and cook for a minute more.

ADD the capers and vinegar and simmer gently for a few minutes to reduce the liquid. Add the parsley just before spreading onto crostini.

CHICKEN LIVER CROSTINI

200 g chicken livers
3 tablespoons olive oil
1 small onion, finely chopped
2 garlic cloves, crushed
1 tablespoon finely chopped sage
2 tablespoons dry Marsala
2 tablespoons mascarpone

TRIM the chicken livers of any sinew. Heat the olive oil in a frying pan and gently cook the onion for 2 minutes until soft. Push the onion to the side, increase the heat and add the livers. Cook until lightly brown on both sides, add the garlic and sage and cook for 1 minute. Add the Marsala and cook briefly to reduce the liquid. Season well. Transfer to a food processor or chop by hand, and blend briefly with the mascarpone. Serve immediately, or chilled, on crostini.

FRITTO MISTO DI MARE

FRITTO MISTO IS TRADITIONALLY A MIXED PLATTER. WE USUALLY THINK OF THIS AS SEAFOOD, AS IN THIS RECIPE, BUT FRITTO MISTO IS ANOTHER OF THOSE ITALIAN DISHES THAT VARIES FROM REGION TO REGION. SOME FAVOUR MEAT OR VEGETABLES, OTHERS USE FRUIT AND EVEN CHOCOLATE.

250 g baby squid
12 large prawns
8 small octopus
16 scallops, cleaned
12 fresh sardines, gutted and
   heads removed
250 g firm white fish fillets (such as
   ling, cod or snapper), skinned and
   cut into large cubes

GARLIC AND ANCHOVY SAUCE
125 ml extra virgin olive oil
2 garlic cloves, crushed
3 anchovy fillets, finely minced
2 tablespoons finely chopped
   parsley
pinch of chilli flakes

BATTER
200 g plain flour
80 ml olive oil
1 large egg white

oil for deep-frying
lemon wedges

SERVES 4

PREHEAT the oven to 140°C (275°F/Gas 1). Clean the squid by pulling the heads and tentacles out of the bodies along with any innards. Cut the heads off below the eyes, just leaving the tentacles. Discard the heads and set the tentacles aside. Rinse the bodies, pulling out the clear quills, and cut the bodies into rings. Peel and devein the prawns, leaving the tails intact.

CLEAN the octopus by slitting the head and pulling out the innards. Cut out the eyes and hard beak and rinse. If the octopus seem a bit big, cut them into halves or quarters.

TO MAKE the sauce, warm the oil in a frying pan. Add the garlic, anchovy, parsley and chilli flakes. Cook over low heat for 1 minute, or until the garlic is soft but not brown. Serve warm or chilled.

TO MAKE the batter, sift the flour into a bowl and stir in ¼ teaspoon salt. Mix in the oil with a wooden spoon, then gradually add 315 ml tepid water, changing to a whisk when the mixture becomes liquid. Continue whisking until the batter is smooth and thick. Stiffly whisk the egg white and fold into the batter. Heat the oil in a deep-fat fryer or deep frying pan to 190°C (375°F), or until a piece of bread fries golden brown in 10 seconds when dropped in the oil.

DRY the seafood on paper towels so the batter will stick. Working with one type of seafood at a time, dip the pieces in batter. Shake off the excess batter, then carefully lower into the oil. Deep-fry for 2–3 minutes, depending on the size of the pieces. Drain on paper towels, then transfer to the oven. Do not crowd the seafood. Keep warm while you fry the remaining seafood.

SERVE the seafood immediately with the lemon wedges and the sauce.

Palermo's wholesale fish market (*Mercato Ittico*) sells fish caught all around Sicily's long coastline.

SEAFOOD ANTIPASTI

THE GOLDEN RULE FOR COOKING SEAFOOD IS THAT ALL YOUR INGREDIENTS MUST BE ABSOLUTELY STRAIGHT-FROM-THE-SEA FRESH. BUY LIVING SHELLFISH FROM THE FISHMONGER AND BE ADVISED AS TO WHAT IS IN SEASON, A REGIONAL SPECIALITY, OR A GOOD CATCH OF THE DAY.

500 g mussels
500 g clams
250 g octopus
250 g small squid
250 g prawns
100 ml olive oil
juice of 2 lemons
2 tablespoons finely chopped
　parsley
lemon wedges

SERVES 6

CLEAN the mussels and clams by scrubbing them thoroughly and scraping off any barnacles. Pull off the beards from the mussels and rinse well under running water. Discard any mussels or clams that are broken or open and do not close when tapped on the work surface.

CLEAN the octopus by slitting the head and pulling out the innards. Cut out the eyes and hard beak and rinse. If the flesh is still springy and has not been tenderized, beat with a mallet until soft.

PREPARE the squid by pulling the heads and tentacles out of the bodies along with any innards. Cut the heads off below the eyes, just leaving the tentacles. Discard the heads and set the tentacles aside. Rinse the bodies, pulling out the clear quills, then cut the bodies into rings. Peel and devein the prawns, leaving the tails intact.

BRING a large pan of water to the boil and add the octopus. Reduce the heat and simmer for about 20 minutes or until tender. Add the squid and prawns. Cook for about 2 minutes, or until the prawns turn pink. Drain well.

PUT the mussels and clams in an even layer in a steamer. Steam over boiling water for 2 minutes or until the shells have just opened (discard any that stay closed). Pull the top shell off each mussel and clam. Arrange on a platter.

IF YOU have one octopus, cut it into pieces; if you have baby ones then leave them whole. Arrange the octopus, squid and prawns on the platter and sprinkle with sea salt and black pepper. Mix the olive oil with the lemon juice and drizzle over the seafood. Cover with clingfilm and leave to marinate in the fridge for at least 2 hours. Before serving, sprinkle with parsley. Serve with lemon wedges and bread to mop up the juices.

Whisking the dressing for the Octopus Salad.

OCTOPUS SALAD

650 g baby octopus
2 tablespoons lemon juice
100 ml olive oil
1 garlic clove, thinly sliced
1 tablespoon chopped mint
1 tablespoon chopped parsley
1 teaspoon Dijon mustard
pinch of cayenne pepper
120 g misticanza (mixed salad
　leaves)
lemon wedges

SERVES 4

CLEAN the octopus by slitting the head and pulling out the innards. Cut out the eyes and hard beak and rinse. If the octopus seem a bit big, cut them into halves or quarters.

BRING a large pan of water to the boil and add the octopus. Simmer for about 8–10 minutes, or until they are tender.

MEANWHILE, make a dressing by mixing together the lemon juice, olive oil, garlic, mint, parsley, mustard and cayenne with some salt and pepper.

DRAIN the octopus well and put in a bowl. Pour the dressing over the top and cool for a few minutes before transferring to the fridge. Chill for at least 3 hours before serving on a bed of misticanza. Drizzle a little of the dressing over the top and serve with lemon wedges.

MARINATED FRESH ANCHOVIES

FRESH ANCHOVIES ARE FISHED ALL OVER THE MEDITERRANEAN, AS WELL AS THE ATLANTIC COASTS OF FRANCE AND SPAIN. YOU WILL NEED VERY FRESH FISH FOR THIS SIMPLE DISH, WITH PERHAPS JUST SOME BREAD TO MOP UP JUICES. THE DISH CAN BE KEPT REFRIGERATED FOR UP TO THREE DAYS.

400 g fresh anchovies
60 ml olive oil
1 tablespoon extra virgin olive oil
3 tablespoons lemon juice
2 garlic cloves, crushed
2 tablespoons finely chopped
　parsley
2 tablespoons finely chopped basil
1 small red chilli, seeded and
　chopped

SERVES 4

FILLET the anchovies by running your thumbnail or a sharp knife along the backbone, then pulling the head upwards. The head, bones and guts should all come away together, leaving you with the fillets. Carefully wash under cold water and pat dry with paper towels. Place the fillets in a shallow serving dish.

MIX ALL the remaining ingredients together with some salt and pepper and pour over the anchovies. Cover with clingfilm and marinate in the fridge for at least 3 hours before serving.

MARINATED FRESH ANCHOVIES

CHARGRILLED OCTOPUS

BUY SMALL OCTOPUS IF YOU CAN FIND THEM—THEY ARE MORE TENDER THAN THE LARGE ONES. IF ONLY LARGE ARE AVAILABLE, TENDERIZE THEM BY BEATING WITH A ROLLING PIN BEFORE COOKING. IN SOME COASTAL REGIONS, YOU CAN SEE OCTOPUS BEING TENDERIZED IN A CEMENT MIXER.

16 small octopus (about 1.5 kg)
175 ml extra virgin olive oil
4 thyme sprigs
2 bay leaves
2 garlic cloves, crushed
lemon wedges

SERVES 4

CLEAN the octopus by slitting the head and pulling out the innards. Cut out the eyes and hard beak and rinse. Skin the octopus tentacles and make small diagonal cuts along their length, cutting about a third of the way through the tentacle. Place in a bowl and pour over the oil. Add the thyme, bay leaves and garlic and toss well. Cover with clingfilm and marinate in the refrigerator overnight. Leave four wooden skewers to soak in water.

HEAT the griddle or a barbecue. Drain the excess oil from the octopus and thread onto the skewers. Cook for 5–7 minutes on each side or until the octopus is golden and the tip of a knife slips through a tentacle. Season with salt and pepper and drizzle with some extra marinade or extra virgin olive oil if you like. Leave for a few minutes and then serve with lemon wedges.

CHARGRILLED OCTOPUS

GARLIC PRAWNS

20 large prawns
60 ml olive oil
80 g butter
1/2 red chilli, finely chopped
10 garlic cloves, crushed
60 ml white wine
3 tablespoons chopped parsley

SERVES 4

PEEL and devein the prawns, leaving the tails intact if you like. Put the olive oil in a large frying pan and add the butter, chilli and half the garlic. Cook, stirring, for 3 minutes. Add the prawns and sprinkle with the remaining garlic.

COOK for 3 minutes or until the prawns are pink. Turn the prawns, add the wine and cook for another 4 minutes. Add the parsley, season well with salt and pepper and serve with bread.

NORCIA in Umbria is famous for its pork butchers and the town gives its name to norcini, a term used throughout Italy to mean pork butchers. Norcini from this area traditionally travelled all over Italy during the butchering and curing season in November to ply their trade, returning home in April. Butcher shops in central Italy that specialize in local cured pork and wild boar products are known as norcineria.

SALUMI

SALUMI IS A GENERAL TERM REFERRING TO ALL ITALY'S FAMOUS CURED OR PRESERVED PORK PRODUCTS, FROM SALAMI AND SALSICCE (SAUSAGES) TO CURED HAMS SUCH AS PARMA, COOKED HAMS SUCH AS PROSCUITTO COTTO, AND INGREDIENTS FROM LARD TO PANCETTA AND COPPA.

Curing meat was once the only way in which meat could be enjoyed all year round. A family would keep a pig to be butchered in the winter, then turn it into salumi to be eaten throughout the year. Though beef, wild boar and venison are used for making cured meats, pork has always predominated, made popular by the fact that every scrap of the animal can be used. When the pig was butchered, the fat would be rendered into lard, the best meat turned into hams and pancetta, the rest of the pig used to make salami and sausages, and the bones saved for stock. The meats would then be cured, usually by drying, smoking or preserving in fat. In Italy, you can still buy just about every part of the pig, including guanciale, cured pig's cheek; trotters, boned and stuffed to make zampone; and the neck, cured and made into coppa.

SALAMI

In Italy, butchers display their salami marked as pork (suino) or beef (bovino), and some may be labelled salsicce rather than salami. A salami can be sold under its own name or marked 'nostrano', meaning that it is from the area or home-

SAN NICOLA'S PARMA HAM is made from pigs' hind legs, preserved by having sea salt massaged into them for a month. The exposed ends are treated with pork fat and the legs air dried in the pure air of the Alta val Parma for a year. Each ham is tested by smell with a piece of bone and any rejects sold as just prosciutto. Certified hams are stamped with the crown of the Duke of Parma and have their birthday written on them.

made. Salami change in flavour and texture according to where they are made. The Northeast tends towards heavier, more Austrian-tasting salami, the Centre prefers a more refined texture, while in the South salami are often spicy. Flavourings may also be added to standard salami — in Tuscany this is often fennel seed and in Umbria truffles are used. The larger the salami, the thinner it should be sliced.

PROSCIUTTO

Prosciutto crudo is a cured ham made from an air-dried pig's leg and sliced paper-thin for antipasto. Parma ham is just one type of prosciutto and many regions produce their own hams. *Prosciutto salato*, salted hams, are cured heavily with salt. Tuscan ham is one of the finest and these robust hams can be excellent with unsalted bread. Parma and San Daniele hams are both *prosciutto dolce*, sweet hams, whose subtle curing and longer hanging give them a sweet, refined flavour.

THIS BUTCHER in Norcia proudly displays its title as an *artigiani norcini* (artisan pork butchers). Nowadays, many norcini work on large pig farms, producing salami and other pork products.

Fresh tuna has a dark meaty flesh that is delicious both raw and cooked. Tuna is fished off the coasts of Sicily and Calabria where the fish come to spawn. The better-tasting red flesh indicates that the tuna was caught by hand, killed and bled quickly, while muddy-brown flesh means the fish drowned and so probably was caught by net.

CARPACCIO

CARPACCIO IS NAMED AFTER THE RENAISSANCE PAINTER WHOSE USE OF REDS IS REFLECTED IN THE DISH. IT WAS CREATED IN HARRY'S BAR IN VENICE FOR A FAVOURITE CUSTOMER WHOSE DOCTOR HAD PLACED HER ON A DIET FORBIDDING COOKED MEAT.

700 g good-quality beef fillet
1 egg yolk
3 teaspoons Dijon mustard
3 tablespoons lemon juice
2 drops Tabasco
75 ml olive oil
1 tablespoon single cream
2–3 tablespoons capers, rinsed

SERVES 6

PLACE the beef in the freezer for about half an hour, or until it is firm. Using a sharp knife or mandolin, cut the beef into paper-thin slices. Cover six serving plates with the beef in an even layer.

BLEND together the egg yolk, mustard, lemon juice and Tabasco in a bowl or food processor. Add the olive oil in a thin stream, whisking or processing continuously until the mayonnaise thickens. Whisk in the cream. Season to taste with salt and pepper. Drizzle over the beef slices and sprinkle with capers.

TUNA CARPACCIO

400 g sashimi-quality tuna
50 g basil leaves
1 garlic clove
80 ml extra virgin olive oil
1 teaspoon lemon juice

SERVES 4

PLACE the tuna in the freezer for about half an hour, or until it is firm. Using a sharp knife or a mandolin, cut the tuna into paper-thin slices. Cover four serving plates with the slices in a thin even layer.

BLANCH the basil leaves in salted boiling water for 10 seconds, then drain well. Place the leaves in a food processor or blender with the garlic, olive oil and lemon juice and mix well. Season with salt and pepper. Drizzle over the tuna and serve with bread.

TUNA CARPACCIO

AFFETTATI MISTI

USE A GOOD SELECTION OF MEATS THAT CONTRAST IN FLAVOUR AND APPEARANCE, BUT STICK TO JUST ONE TYPE OF FRUIT. INSTEAD OF MELON OR FIGS YOU COULD TRY THIN SLICES OF PEAR, AND BLACK OLIVES INSTEAD OF GREEN ARE FINE.

8 slices mortadella
8 slices prosciutto
12 slices coppa
15 slices bresaola (air-dried beef)
15–20 slices casalinga (coarse)
   salami or finocchiona (Tuscan
   salami with fennel seeds)
young rocket leaves
lemon wedges
extra virgin olive oil
quartered fresh figs or slices of
   honeydew melon or cantaloupe
pickled onions or cipolline
   agrodolce (page 26)
green olives
cetriolini (small gherkins)
'country-style' bread, such as
   ciabatta

SERVES 6

ARRANGE the meat around a large platter. Vary the presentation by rolling up the mortadella, for instance, or folding large salami slices into a half-moon shape. Use the rocket as a bed for the coppa or bresaola.

PLACE the lemon wedges by the prosciutto and drizzle extra virgin olive oil over the bresaola. Arrange the figs or slices of melon next to the prosciutto.

SERVE the onions, olives and cetriolini separately in bowls, and provide plenty of sliced bread. Also have on hand the bottle of extra virgin olive oil and plenty of black pepper.

Italian cured meat is very much regionally based, with each area making its own affettati misti. If you are putting together an antipasti platter, you can match up local products—try Parma ham with mortadella and a local Bolognese salami. For the best flavour, slice large salami and meat very thinly.

GRILLED TOMATOES

4 large ripe tomatoes
2 garlic cloves, crushed
60 ml olive oil
1 tablespoon chopped parsley

SERVES 4

CUT the tomatoes in half horizontally. Place them on a baking tray, skin side up, and grill them for 2 minutes, then turn. Mix together the garlic, olive oil and parsley and drizzle over the tomatoes. Season with salt and pepper.

PLACE the tomatoes back under the grill and cook for 6 minutes or until cooked. Serve hot or warm.

GRILLED TOMATOES

PINZIMONIO

8 spring onions
4 young Romanesco or Violetto
  Toscano artichokes
2 tablespoons lemon juice
2 baby fennel bulbs
8 celery stalks
8 red or white radishes
8 baby carrots
1 red pepper
200 ml extra virgin olive oil

SERVES 4

TRIM the spring onions at both ends. Cut off and discard the top third of each artichoke and the tough outer leaves, and snip off any spikes from the remaining leaves. Trim the stem and peel with a potato peeler.

SLICE EACH artichoke in half and scrape out the furry choke and discard. Place the artichokes in a bowl of lemon water to avoid discolouring. Trim the tops of the fennel and cut into quarters. Trim the celery and radishes. Peel the carrots leaving any greenery attached. Cut the red pepper into strips. Arrange the vegetables on a platter.

DIVIDE the oil among four small dishes and season with salt and pepper. Give each person a dish of oil to dip the vegetables into.

BAGNA CAODA

A FONDUE BOWL AND BURNER WORKS VERY WELL TO HEAT THE BAGNA CAODA (THE NAME MEANS LITERALLY 'HOT BATH'). THIS PIEMONTESE SPECIALITY IS A POPULAR GROUP MEAL ALL YEAR ROUND, BUT IS ESPECIALLY ASSOCIATED WITH THE VIBRANT ATMOSPHERE OF THE GRAPE HARVEST.

40 pieces assorted raw vegetables
  (carrot, celery, spring onion,
  fennel or cauliflower florets)
200 ml olive oil
6 garlic cloves, crushed
120 g anchovy fillets, finely minced
90 g butter
'country-style' bread, such as
  ciabatta

SERVES 4

TRIM, wash and dry the vegetables and cut them into strips for dipping.

PUT the oil, garlic and anchovies in a saucepan and place over moderately low heat. Cook gently, stirring once or twice, until the anchovies dissolve. Do not let the garlic brown. Add the butter and leave over low heat until it has melted. Season with pepper.

TRANSFER the sauce to a bowl and keep warm at the table by placing on a food warmer or over a burner or spirit stove. Serve the vegetables and bread arranged on a platter. Guests dip their choice of vegetable into the bagna caôda and use a piece of bread to catch any stray drips.

BAGNA CAODA

CAPONATA

1 kg aubergines
1/2 tablespoon salt
220 ml olive oil
1 large onion, roughly chopped
2 celery stalks, sliced
1 small red pepper, cut into short
  strips
2 tablespoons pine nuts
400 g tin chopped tomatoes
4 tablespoons red wine vinegar
1 tablespoon sugar
2 tablespoons capers, rinsed and
  chopped if large
24 green olives, pitted and halved
4 tablespoons finely chopped
  parsley

SERVES 6

CUT the aubergines into 2 cm cubes and place in layers in a colander, sprinkling each layer with salt as you go. Leave to drain for 30 minutes. Rinse and squeeze the aubergine dry with your hands.

HEAT 90 ml of the oil in a large frying pan. Brown the aubergine in batches over high heat, adding oil as needed. Drain on paper towels.

ADD MORE oil to the pan, reduce the heat and cook the onion and celery for 5 minutes, or until softened but not brown. Add the red pepper and pine nuts and cook for 2 minutes. Spoon off any excess oil and add the tomatoes and 60 ml water. Simmer for 10 minutes or until the mixture is quite dry. Season well with black pepper.

ADD the vinegar, sugar, capers and olives and cook for 2–3 minutes over low heat. Add the aubergine, cook for a further 5–6 minutes, then remove from the heat and leave to cool. Taste for pepper and toss the parsley through to serve.

Olive oil and red wine vinegar are found on every restaurant table in Italy to dress your salad, as well as being used together in a multitude of dishes. The acidity of the wine vinegar cuts through the oiliness.

PANZANELLA

1 garlic clove, cut in half
1 loaf 'country-style' bread, such as
  ciabatta
6 ripe tomatoes
1 small yellow pepper
1/2 cucumber, peeled
1/2 white salad onion
2 tablespoons shredded basil
  leaves
90 ml olive oil
2 tablespoons red wine vinegar

SERVES 4

RUB the cut side of the garlic around the inside of a large salad bowl. Remove the crust from the bread and cut it into cubes. Put the bread in the bowl and sprinkle it with enough cold water to moisten.

CUT the tomatoes, pepper and cucumber into chunks and dice the onion. Add the vegetables to the bread with the basil and then sprinkle with the olive oil and vinegar. Toss well and leave for 30 minutes before serving.

PANZANELLA

CHARGRILLED AUBERGINE SALAD

2 large aubergines, thinly sliced
  lengthways
2 garlic cloves, crushed
150 ml extra virgin olive oil
juice of 1 small lemon
1/2 red chilli, finely chopped
15 g basil or mint leaves, roughly
  chopped

SERVES 4

HEAT a griddle on the stove and cook the aubergine, a few slices at a time, over moderately high heat, turning once until it is soft and cooked. (There is no need to add oil or to salt the aubergine first.) As you remove the aubergine slices from the griddle, put them on a plate on top of each other—this helps them to steam a little and soften further.

IF you do not have a griddle, preheat the oven to 200°C (400°F/Gas 6). Drizzle a couple of tablespoons of olive oil over a baking tray and place the aubergine slices on top. Drizzle with a little more oil and cook the aubergine until soft.

MIX TOGETHER the garlic, olive oil, lemon juice, chilli and herbs. (If you have baked the aubergine, use a little less oil.) Place the aubergine in a flat dish and pour over the marinade. Mix briefly without breaking up the aubergine and marinate for at least 30 minutes before serving.

CHARGRILLED VEGETABLE SALAD

4 long thin aubergines
4 courgettes
4 plum tomatoes
1 small red pepper
1 small green pepper
1 small yellow pepper
60 ml olive oil
2 garlic cloves, halved

DRESSING
60 ml extra virgin olive oil
1 tablespoon balsamic vinegar
1 garlic clove, crushed
3 tablespoons chopped parsley
1/4 teaspoon caster sugar

SERVES 4

SLICE the aubergines and courgettes diagonally into 1 cm thick pieces. Halve the tomatoes lengthways and slice the peppers into short strips. Place all the vegetables in a bowl and add the olive oil and the garlic. Toss well.

PREHEAT a griddle and brush with oil. Cook the aubergine and courgette for 2–4 minutes on each side, or until browned. Transfer to a shallow serving dish. Cook the tomatoes and peppers for 1–2 minutes on each side, or until the peppers start to smell sweet and their skins blister. Transfer to the serving dish and set aside to cool.

TO MAKE the dressing, mix together all the ingredients and then season. Drizzle the dressing over the vegetables and toss lightly. Serve at room temperature.

CHARGRILLED
VEGETABLE SALAD

INSALATA CAPRESE

INSALATA CAPRESE IS TRADITIONALLY SERVED WITH NO OTHER DRESSING THAN A DRIZZLE OF EXTRA VIRGIN OLIVE OIL. HOWEVER, IF YOU'RE NOT ABSOLUTELY CONFIDENT THAT YOUR TOMATOES HAVE THE BEST FLAVOUR, A LITTLE BALSAMIC VINEGAR WILL HELP THEM ALONG.

6 ripe plum tomatoes
3–4 balls mozzarella
2 tablespoons extra virgin olive oil
15 young basil leaves
1/2 teaspoon balsamic vinegar
(optional)

SERVES 4

SLICE the tomatoes, pouring off any excess juice, and cut the mozzarella into slices of a similar thickness.

ARRANGE alternating rows of tomato and mozzarella on a serving plate. Sprinkle with salt and pepper and drizzle the olive oil over the top. Tear the basil leaves into pieces and scatter over the oil. To serve, take to the table and sprinkle with the balsamic vinegar, if you're using it.

INSALATA DI RINFORZO

250 g carrots
150 g green beans
1/2 red onion
600 ml white wine vinegar
1 tablespoon sea salt
1 tablespoon sugar
1 bay leaf
300 g cauliflower florets

DRESSING
80 ml extra virgin olive oil
2 tablespoons lemon juice
1 tablespoon finely chopped parsley
1 tablespoon chopped capers
1 garlic clove, halved

4 anchovy fillets, halved lengthways
85 g small black olives, such as
Ligurian
1 tablespoon roughly chopped
parsley
1–2 tablespoons extra virgin olive oil

SERVES 4

CUT the carrots into lengths the size of your little finger, slice the beans into similar lengths and slice the onion into rings.

COMBINE the vinegar, salt, sugar and bay leaf in a saucepan with 500 ml water and bring to the boil. Cook the carrots for about 3 minutes until just tender. Transfer to a bowl with a slotted spoon. Add the beans to the pan and cook for about 2 minutes until similarly done. Add to the carrots in the bowl. Add the onion and cauliflower to the pan and cook for about 3 minutes until the cauliflower just starts to soften. Drain, add to the bowl and cool.

TO MAKE the dressing, mix together the olive oil, lemon juice, parsley, capers and garlic and season well. Pour over the cooled vegetables and toss gently. The salad can be stored in an airtight container for up to 2 weeks at this stage.

TO SERVE toss through the anchovy fillets, olives, parsley and oil.

Caprese is also known as *insalata tricolore* — the mozzarella, ripe tomatoes and basil reflect the colours of the Italian flag.

INSALATA DI RINFORZO

PARMIGIANO REGGIANO is made daily at the Coop. Casearia Castelnovese using milk from all over Modena. The milk is brought to the cooperative by each farm, then left to stand so the cream comes to the top and can be skimmed off. One thousand litres of both this skimmed and some unskimmed milk is then poured into one of the cooperative's huge copper cauldrons, rennet is added and the milk heated to form

CHEESE

AS WELL AS MAKING FAMOUS CHEESES LIKE PARMIGIANO REGGIANO OR MOZZARELLA, ITALIAN CHEESEMAKERS CREATE HUNDREDS OF REGIONAL CHEESES, FRESH AND AGED, AND MANY NEVER FOUND OUTSIDE ITALY.

The history of cheese in Italy is very closely related to the country's varied geography. The rich mountainous pastures of the North produce hundreds of cheeses like fontina, Gorgonzola, mascarpone, Asiago, grana padano and Taleggio. In the Centre, Emilia-Romagna is the home of Parmigiano Reggiano (Parmesan), perhaps Italy's most famous cheese. Tuscany and Umbria produce fresh pecorinos, while the sparser and hotter South is more suited

to farming sheep and goats than cows. These sheep and goats' cheeses are usually harder than the French *chèvre* and are even suitable for grating, though you can also find soft, fresh cheeses like sheep's ricotta. The South is also the home of *pasta filata*, cheeses made from stretched out curds like mozzarella, scamorza, caciocavallo and provolone. In Campania, buffalo milk is used to make mozzarella.

DENOMINAZIONE DI ORIGINE CONTROLLATA

Many of the traditional methods for making cheese are safeguarded by *consorzi* (cooperatives), who have imposed their own rules for production to ensure that their cheeses are made to the highest quality, using the best milk in each area. The rules for production can include methods passed down through centuries, such as milking Parmesan cows by hand, and this explains the often higher cost of these cheeses. Cheeses from these cooperatives are usually awarded a DOC (*Denominazione di Origine Controllata*) rating in the form of a brand or stamp on the rind.

When a crust begins to form, the cheese is wrapped in a sheet of plastic that imprints the brand number and Parmigiano Reggiano stamp onto its rind, while a metal band over the top holds the shape. After being branded, the cheeses are placed in saline for three days, then arranged on wooden shelves to dry. The drying process take place in a huge room called a cathedral, where the cheeses are left to mature for up to a

curds. After cutting the curds into tiny pieces, the mixture is heated further until the curds collect together again at the bottom of the cauldron. When this has happened, they are scooped up into a linen cloth. Extremely heavy, the curds must be cut into two cheeses, each one wrapped in its own cloth to drain. The new cheeses are lifted into white moulds to be shaped, then turned every few hours for one day.

MILK FOR CHEESE

Italian cheeses can be made from cows', buffaloes', goats' and sheep's milk. Cows' milk is used more in the North, while buffaloes are just farmed around Naples and almost all the milk is used for *mozzarella di bufala* (although most mozzarella production in Italy is now in fact made with cheaper cows' milk). Goats' and sheep's cheeses are increasingly popular, and most are produced in Tuscany, Umbria and the South. Both pasteurized and unpasteurized cheeses are made in Italy, with unpasteurized or partly unpasteurized cheeses, such as caciocavallo and provolone, being known as *pasta cruda* and continuing to develop as they age.

HARD AND SOFT CHEESES

Italian cheeses are also divided into hard and soft cheeses. Hard cheeses (*formaggi a pasta dura*) have a water content of less than 40 per cent and include cheeses used mainly for cooking like grana padano and pecorino. Soft cheeses

(*formaggi a pasta molle*) have a water content of more than 40 per cent and are best eaten as soon as possible after being made. They include cheeses like mascarpone and mozzarella, which should be eaten the day they are made.

Unlike French cheeses, Italian cheeses are more famous worldwide for their use in cooking than for being eaten as a separate cheese course. In Italy though, cheeses are often eaten at every course, in cooking and as table cheeses. Cooking cheeses are known as *formaggio per cucina* and perhaps the most famous is Parmigiano Reggiano, rarely eaten as part of a cheese platter outside of Italy. Table cheeses are known as *formaggio da tavola* and, in Italy, both fresh and hard cheeses are eaten on their own. A piece of Parmigiano Reggiano eaten with just a fresh fig or thinly sliced prosciutto; a ball of fresh buffalo mozzarella with some very ripe tomatoes and basil; or a tub of fresh ricotta sweetened with a little honey are some of the simplest and most delicious treats to be had in Italian cuisine.

year, while being turned and cleaned every few days by robots. There are strict rules covering the quality of the cheeses, and before they can be sold they are tested by experts, who tap each cheese to listen for 'faults' inside. A faulty cheese is marked with a cross and sold young. If a cheese passes the test, it can be branded as DOC. Parmesan are never cut, but instead are cracked open by pushing small knives into the rind.

MINESTRONE ALLA GENOVESE

JUST ABOUT EVERY REGION OF ITALY HAS ITS OWN MINESTRONE. THIS VERSION HAS A SPOONFUL OF PESTO STIRRED THROUGH AT THE END; OTHERS HAVE RICE INSTEAD OF PASTA. FOR *MINESTRONE ALLA MILANESE*, ADD 200 GRAMS ARBORIO RICE INSTEAD OF THE PASTA.

220 g dried borlotti beans
50 g lard or butter
1 large onion, finely chopped
1 garlic clove, finely chopped
15 g parsley, finely chopped
2 sage leaves
100 g pancetta, cubed
2 celery stalks, halved then sliced
2 carrots, sliced
3 potatoes, peeled but left whole
1 teaspoon tomato purée
400 g tin chopped tomatoes
8 basil leaves
3 litres chicken or vegetable stock
2 courgettes, sliced
220 g shelled peas
120 g runner beans, cut into 4 cm
  lengths
1/4 cabbage, shredded
150 g ditalini, avemarie or other
  small pasta
1 quantity pesto (page 285)
grated Parmesan

SERVES 6

PUT the dried beans in a large bowl, cover with cold water and leave to soak overnight. Drain and rinse under cold water.

TO MAKE the *soffritto*, melt the lard in a large saucepan and add the onion, garlic, parsley, sage and pancetta. Cook over low heat, stirring once or twice, for about 10 minutes, or until the onion is soft and golden.

ADD the celery, carrot and potatoes and cook for 5 minutes. Stir in the tomato purée, tomatoes, basil and borlotti beans. Season with plenty of pepper. Add the stock and bring slowly to the boil. Cover and leave to simmer for 2 hours, stirring once or twice.

IF the potatoes haven't already broken up, roughly break them up with a fork against the side of the pan. Taste for seasoning and add the courgette, peas, runner beans, cabbage and pasta. Simmer until the pasta is *al dente*. Serve with a dollop of pesto and the Parmesan.

The soup base is called a *soffritto*, which means 'underfried'. The slow-cooked mixture of onion, garlic, pancetta and herbs gives the soup its base flavour. Other types of minestrone simmer the vegetables in stock without frying them first, then add olive oil towards the end for flavour.

ZUPPA DI PESCE

FOR A COUNTRY WHERE ALMOST EVERY REGION HAS A SEA COAST, IT IS HARDLY SURPRISING THAT ITALY HAS ALMOST AS MANY VERSIONS OF THIS SOUP AS THERE ARE FISH IN THE SEA. THIS RECIPE INCLUDES SUGGESTIONS FOR FISH VARIETIES, BUT ASK YOUR FISHMONGER WHAT'S BEST ON THE DAY.

Score a criss-cross pattern into the squid to make it curl.

FISH STOCK
300 g firm white fish fillets, such as monkfish, red mullet, cod, deep sea perch, skinned and cut into large cubes, bones reserved
12 prawns
1 small onion, roughly chopped
1 carrot, roughly chopped
15 g parsley, roughly chopped, stalks reserved

200 g squid tubes
4 tablespoons olive oil
1 onion, finely chopped
1 celery stalk, finely chopped
1 carrot, finely chopped
2 garlic cloves, finely chopped
pinch of cayenne pepper
1 fennel bulb, trimmed and thinly sliced
125 ml dry white wine
400 g tin chopped tomatoes
250 g scallops, cleaned

CROSTINI
3 tablespoons extra virgin olive oil
2 garlic cloves, crushed
4 slices 'country-style' bread, such as ciabatta

SERVES 4

TO MAKE the fish stock, rinse the fish bones in cold water, removing any blood or intestines. Peel and devein the prawns and put the fish bones and prawn shells in a large saucepan with just enough water to cover. Bring slowly to a simmer, skimming any froth from the surface. Add the onion, carrot and the stalks from the parsley, then simmer gently for 20 minutes. Strain through a fine colander and measure 1.5 litres stock. If there is less than this, add a little water; if there is more than this, put the strained stock back into the saucepan and simmer until reduced to 1.5 litres.

LIE the squid out flat, skin side up, and score a criss-cross pattern into the flesh, being careful not to cut all the way through. Slice diagonally into bite-sized strips.

HEAT the oil in a large saucepan and cook the onion, celery, carrot, garlic and chopped parsley over moderately low heat for 5–6 minutes, or until softened but not browned.

ADD the cayenne pepper and season well. Stir in the fennel and cook for 2–3 minutes. Add the white wine, increase the heat and cook until it has been absorbed. Stir in the tomatoes, then add the fish stock and bring to the boil. Reduce the heat and simmer for 20 minutes.

ADD the squid to the pan with the fish pieces and simmer for 1 minute. Add the scallops and prawns and simmer for a further 2 minutes. Taste and add more seasoning if necessary.

TO MAKE the crostini, heat the olive oil and crushed garlic in a large frying pan over moderately low heat. Add the slices of bread and fry on both sides until golden. Place a slice of bread into each of four warmed serving bowls. Ladle the soup on top and serve immediately.

LA RIBOLLITA

RIBOLLITA MEANS 'REBOILED' BECAUSE THIS TUSCAN BEAN SOUP IS BEST MADE A DAY IN ADVANCE TO LET THE FLAVOURS DEVELOP, THEN REHEATED. IT SHOULD THEN BE THICK ENOUGH TO EAT WITH A FORK RATHER THAN A SPOON.

4 tablespoons olive oil
1 onion, finely chopped
1 large carrot, finely chopped
3 celery stalks, finely chopped
2 large garlic cloves, crushed
250 g cavolo nero or savoy
   cabbage
1 courgette, finely chopped
400 g cooked cannellini or borlotti
   beans
400 g tin tomatoes
200 ml red wine
1 litre chicken stock or water
75 g stale 'country-style' bread,
   such as ciabatta or pugliese,
   crusts removed and broken into
   2.5 cm cubes
drizzle of extra virgin olive oil

SERVES 4

TO MAKE the *soffritto*, pour the olive oil into a large saucepan and add the onion. Cook the onion gently—use this time to chop the carrot and celery and add them to the pan as you go along. Once you have added the garlic, leave to cook for a few minutes.

STRIP the leaves of the cavolo from the stems or cut away the thick stem of the savoy. Wash and finely chop the stems and roughly chop the leaves. Add the cabbage stems and courgette to the *soffritto* and cook, stirring occasionally, for about 5 minutes, or until the vegetables have changed to an opaque colour and soaked up some of the olive oil.

STIR in the beans and cook for 5 minutes more, then add the tomatoes and cook for a further 5 minutes to reduce the liquid.

ADD the cabbage leaves and mix into the soup, stirring until just wilted. Add the wine and stock or water and gently simmer for about 40 minutes.

ADD the bread to the pan (if the bread is very fresh, dry it out a little in the oven first to prevent it disintegrating into the soup). Mix briefly and remove the pan from the heat. Leave for about 30 minutes. This rests the soup and allows the flavours to mingle. Serve hot but not boiling with a generous drizzle of extra virgin olive oil.

IF REHEATING the soup, make sure it comes to the boil but then remove it from the heat and leave to cool for 5 minutes. Serve in cold bowls. The soup should be warm, rather than piping hot.

Make sure the cabbage stems are thoroughly softened before adding the other vegetables—this gives the cabbage a chance to really soak up the flavour of the *soffritto*.

CHESTNUT, PANCETTA AND CABBAGE SOUP

100 g cavolo nero or savoy
   cabbage, roughly chopped
2 tablespoons olive oil
1 large onion, finely chopped
185 g pancetta, diced
3 garlic cloves, crushed
10 g rosemary, chopped
300 g cooked peeled chestnuts
150 ml red wine
drizzle of extra virgin olive oil

SERVES 4

COOK the cabbage in 1.5 litres boiling salted water for about 10 minutes. Drain, reserving the water. Rinse the cabbage in cold water if too hot to handle, and chop more finely.

HEAT the olive oil in a large saucepan and cook the onion and pancetta over moderately high heat until the onion is soft and the pancetta lightly browned. Add the garlic and rosemary and cook for a few minutes. Break up the chestnuts a little and add to the pan with the cabbage. Stir to infuse the flavours, season, then add the wine. Bring to the boil and cook for a couple of minutes. Finally add the cabbage water and simmer for about 15 minutes.

PUREE HALF of the soup, leaving the remainder unpuréed to create a little texture. Serve hot with a drizzle of extra virgin olive oil over each bowl.

Spoleto town centre.

Farro is a grain also known as 'spelt'. It was widely used by the Romans to make porridge, soups and, in its ground form, bread.

MINESTRA DI FARRO

200 g dried borlotti beans
2 tablespoons olive oil
1 small onion, thinly sliced
2 garlic cloves, crushed
1.5 litres chicken stock
8 mint leaves, roughly torn
200 g farro (spelt)
100 g Parmesan, grated
1 tablespoon finely chopped mint
4 teaspoons extra virgin olive oil

SERVES 4

SOAK the borlotti beans in cold water overnight. Drain and place in a large saucepan with plenty of cold water. Bring to the boil and simmer until tender (about 1¹/₂ hours, depending on the age of the beans). Drain.

HEAT the olive oil in a large saucepan and cook the onion over low heat for 6 minutes, or until soft. Season. Add the garlic and cook without browning for 20–30 seconds. Add the stock and torn mint and bring to the boil.

STIR in the farro a little at a time so that the stock continues to boil, then lower the heat and simmer for 15 minutes. Add the borlotti beans and simmer for 30 minutes, or until the farro is tender and the soup thick. Purée half the soup. Return to the pan and stir in the Parmesan and chopped mint. Season and stir in 125–250 ml hot water to give a spoonable consistency. Serve immediately, with a teaspoon of extra virgin olive oil stirred through each bowl.

MINESTRA DI FARRO

ZUPPA DI VERDURE

3 tablespoons olive oil
2 small onions, chopped
2 celery stalks, chopped
4 small carrots, chopped
2 large potatoes, diced
2 leeks, sliced
2 garlic cloves, crushed
100 g runner beans
100 g shelled green peas
1.75 litres vegetable stock
150 g cavolo nero or cabbage
12 asparagus spears
6 slices 'country-style' bread, such
    as ciabatta, crusts removed
1 garlic clove, cut in half
40 g Parmesan, grated
drizzle of extra virgin olive oil

SERVES 6

HEAT the olive oil in a large saucepan and add the onion, celery, carrot, potato, leek and crushed garlic. Cook over low heat for 5–6 minutes, or until the vegetables are softened but not browned. Season, add 375 ml water and bring to the boil. Reduce to low heat and simmer for 30 minutes.

SLICE the beans diagonally and add to the pan. Add the peas and stock and simmer for a further 30 minutes. Finely shred the cabbage and slice the asparagus diagonally. Add both to the pan and simmer for a further 5 minutes.

TOAST the bread and, while still hot, rub on both sides with the cut edge of the halved garlic clove.

STIR the Parmesan into the soup and taste for seasoning. Place a slice of toast in the bottom of each bowl and ladle the soup over the top. Drizzle with a little olive oil and serve at once.

PAPPA AL POMODORO

PAPPA AL POMODORO IS A TUSCAN SOUP MADE, AS SO MANY GREAT ITALIAN DISHES ARE, TO USE UP LEFTOVERS—IN THIS CASE BREAD AND TOMATOES. *PAPPA* MEANS 'MUSH' AND THAT IS THE SOUP'S CONSISTENCY. PAPPA AL POMODORO IS A VARIETY OF *PANCOTTO,* BREAD SOUP.

2 tablespoons olive oil
3 garlic cloves, crushed
1 white onion, finely chopped
900 g ripe tomatoes, peeled and
    finely chopped
200 g stale 'country-style' bread,
    such as ciabatta, thickly sliced
    and crusts removed
840 ml hot chicken stock
20 basil leaves, shredded
drizzle of extra virgin olive oil

SERVES 4

HEAT the olive oil in a large saucepan. Add the garlic and onion and cook over low heat for 6–8 minutes, or until softened but not browned. Add the tomatoes and season. Cover and simmer for 30 minutes. Break the bread into pieces and add to the saucepan. Simmer, stirring once or twice, for 5 minutes.

GRADUALLY stir in the stock. Cook, stirring, until the bread has broken down and the soup is thick. Remove from the heat and add the basil. Cover and leave for 1 hour. Serve at room temperature or reheat. Drizzle extra virgin olive oil into each bowl before serving.

PAPPA AL POMODORO

ARTICHOKE FRITTATA

ALMOST AN OMELETTE, BUT FLASHED UNDER THE GRILL TO FINISH OFF THE COOKING, THE FRITTATA
VARIES FROM THIN AND PANCAKE-LIKE, TO THICKER, WITH A GOLDEN CRUST AND CREAMY CENTRE. IT
IS A FAVOURITE THROUGHOUT ITALY, BUT THE ARTICHOKE FRITTATA IS A SPECIALITY OF TRENTINO.

175 g broad beans, fresh or frozen
1 onion
400 g tin artichoke hearts, drained
3 tablespoons olive oil
6 eggs
2 tablespoons chopped parsley
45 g pecorino, grated
pinch of nutmeg

SERVES 4

BRING a small saucepan of water to the boil and
add a large pinch of salt and the broad beans.
Boil for 2 minutes, then drain and rinse under cold
water. Peel off the skins from the beans.

HALVE the onion and slice thinly. Cut the
artichoke hearts from bottom to top into slices
about 5 mm wide. Discard any slices that contain
the tough central choke.

HEAT the oil in a 30 cm frying pan and fry the
onion over low heat for 6–8 minutes, without
allowing it to brown. Add the artichoke slices and
cook for 1–2 minutes. Stir in the broad beans.

PREHEAT the grill. Lightly beat together the eggs,
parsley, pecorino and nutmeg and season well
with salt and pepper. Pour into the frying pan and
cook over low heat until three-quarters set,
shaking the pan often to stop the frittata sticking.

FINISH the top off under the grill and leave to cool
before serving in wedges.

Preparing artichokes by hand at
the Rialto market in Venice.

RED PEPPER AND COURGETTE FRITTATA

1 tablespooon olive oil
1 onion, sliced
1 red pepper, sliced
2 courgettes, sliced
6 eggs
1 tablespoon chopped basil
45 g Parmesan, grated

SERVES 4

HEAT the olive oil in a 30 cm frying pan and cook
the onion until soft. Add the red pepper and
courgette and fry until soft. Preheat the grill.

LIGHTLY beat the eggs, basil and Parmesan and
season well. Pour into the frying pan and cook over
low heat until three-quarters set, shaking the pan to
stop the frittata sticking. Finish the top off under
the grill and leave to cool before serving in wedges.

The courgette is one of Italy's
favourite vegetables. In the north it
is baked in béchamel, in the south
fried with tomatoes and basil.
These long ones are from Sicily.

ARTICHOKE FRITTATA WITH RED PEPPER AND COURGETTE FRITTATA

OMELETTE WITH FRESH HERBS AND PARMESAN

1 tablespoon butter
1¹/2 tablespoons olive oil
6 eggs
2 tablespoons finely chopped mixed
  basil, parsley and chives
20 g Parmesan shavings

SERVES 2

HEAT the butter and oil in a small frying pan. Beat the eggs and stir in the herbs. Season well.

POUR the eggs into the frying pan and cook gently over high heat, pulling the mixture in from the sides until it begins to set in small, fluffy clumps. Reduce the heat and shake the pan from side to side to prevent the omelette sticking.

WHEN the omelette is almost set but still soft on the surface, scatter the Parmesan onto one half and fold the other half over to encase it. Cook for a further 10–12 seconds, shaking the pan once or twice. Slide onto a warm plate and serve at once.

COURGETTE AND
PARMESAN OMELETTE

COURGETTE AND PARMESAN OMELETTE

¹/2 tablespoon butter
1 tablespoon olive oil
1 small courgette, sliced
1 small leek, white part only, sliced
small pinch of nutmeg
¹/2 teaspoon finely chopped basil

1 tablespoon butter
1¹/2 tablespoons olive oil
6 eggs
20 g Parmesan shavings

SERVES 2

HEAT the butter and olive oil in a small frying pan. Gently fry the courgette and leek for 5–6 minutes, or until golden. Season with salt, pepper and the nutmeg, stir in the basil and remove from the pan.

MAKE the omelette as above (without the herbs). Spoon the courgette and leek mix on top of the Parmesan, then fold the omelette over to encase it. Cook for a further 10–12 seconds, shaking the pan once or twice. Slide onto a warm plate and serve at once.

MUSHROOM AND
FENNEL OMELETTE

MUSHROOM AND FENNEL OMELETTE

2 tablespoons butter
100 g button mushrooms, sliced
1 baby fennel bulb, thinly sliced
  (reserving the fronds)

1 tablespoon butter
1¹/2 tablespoons olive oil
6 eggs

SERVES 2

HEAT the butter in a small frying pan and cook the mushrooms and fennel for 4–5 minutes, until the fennel has softened and the mushrooms are lightly golden. Season and remove from the pan. Make the omelette as above, using 1¹/2 tablespoons of chopped fennel fronds instead of the herbs. Spoon the mushroom mix onto one half, then fold the omelette over. Cook for 10–12 seconds, shaking the pan once or twice. Slide onto a warm plate and serve at once.

SUPPLI

WHEN THESE CROQUETTES ARE BITTEN INTO, THE MOZZARELLA PULLS OUT TO RESEMBLE STRANDS OF TELEPHONE WIRES, HENCE THE ITALIAN NAME FOR THIS DISH, *SUPPLI AL TELEFONO*. SUPPLI ARE EXCELLENT FOR USING UP LEFTOVER RISOTTO.

3 tablespoons butter
1 small onion, finely chopped
1.5 litres chicken stock
400 g risotto rice (vialone nano,
    arborio or carnaroli)
75 g Parmesan, grated
2 eggs, beaten
9 basil leaves, torn in half
150 g mozzarella, cut into
    18 cubes (about 1.5 cm square)
150 g dried breadcrumbs
oil for deep-frying

SERVES 6

MELT the butter in a large saucepan. Add the onion and cook over low heat for 3–4 minutes until softened but not browned. Heat the stock to simmering point in another saucepan.

ADD the rice to the onion and cook, stirring, for 1 minute to seal the rice. Add several ladles of the hot stock, stirring continuously so that the rice cooks evenly. Keep adding enough stock to just cover the rice, stirring frequently. Continue in this way for about 20 minutes, or until the rice is creamy on the outside but still *al dente*.

REMOVE from the heat and stir in the Parmesan and eggs. Season with salt and pepper. Spread out on a large baking tray to cool completely.

DIVIDE the rice into 18 portions. Take one portion in the palm of your hand and place a piece of basil and a cube of mozzarella in the centre. Fold the rice over to encase the cheese and at the same time mould the croquette into an egg shape. Roll the croquette in breadcrumbs and place on a baking tray while you make the rest.

HEAT enough oil in a deep-fat fryer or deep frying pan to fully cover the croquettes. Heat the oil to 180°C (350°F), or until a piece of bread fries golden brown in 15 seconds when dropped in the oil. Deep-fry the suppli in batches, without crowding, for about 4 minutes, or until evenly golden brown. Drain on paper towels and serve at once, as they are or with a fresh tomato sauce (page 285).

Shaping the suppli takes a little practice but, if the rice is the right consistency, it is fairly easy. Make sure the basil and mozzarella filling is fully enclosed so it doesn't spill out when the suppli are fried.

ARANCINI

ARANCINI—THE NAME MEANS 'LITTLE ORANGES'—ARE A SPECIALITY OF SICILY. THE SAFFRON RISOTTO IS TRADITIONAL. IF YOU CAN FIND IT, USE VIALONE NANO OR ANOTHER SEMI-FINE RICE—THE GLUTINOUS TEXTURE KEEPS THE GRAINS OF RICE TOGETHER.

large pinch of saffron threads
250 ml white wine
100 g butter
1 onion, finely chopped
1 large garlic clove, crushed
750 ml chicken stock
2 tablespoons thyme
225 g risotto rice (vialone nano,
   arborio or carnaroli)
50 g Parmesan, grated

100 g mozzarella or fontina, cut into
   cubes
75 g dried breadcrumbs
oil for deep-frying

MAKES 20

LEAVE the saffron to soak in the wine while you prepare the risotto. Melt the butter in a large saucepan. Add the onion and garlic and cook over low heat for 3–4 minutes until softened but not browned. Heat the stock to simmering point in another saucepan.

ADD the thyme and rice to the onion and cook, stirring, for 1 minute to seal the rice. Add the wine and saffron and stir until the wine is all absorbed. Add several ladles of the hot stock, stirring continuously so that the rice cooks evenly. Keep adding enough stock to just cover the rice, stirring frequently. Continue in this way for about 20 minutes, or until the rice is creamy.

FOR ARANCINI it is not so essential to keep the rice *al dente*. Add more water or chicken stock if the rice is not fully cooked. Make sure all this liquid is absorbed. Remove from the heat and stir in the Parmesan, then spread out onto a tray covered with clingfilm. Leave to cool and, if possible, leave in the fridge overnight.

TO MAKE the arancini, roll a small amount of risotto into a walnut-sized ball. Press a hole in the middle with your thumb, place a small piece of cheese inside and press the risotto around it to enclose in a ball. Repeat with the rest of the risotto. Roll each ball in the breadcrumbs, pressing down to coat well.

HEAT enough oil in a deep-fat fryer or deep frying pan to fully cover the arancini. Heat the oil to 180°C (350°F), or until a piece of bread fries golden brown in 15 seconds when dropped in the oil. Deep-fry the arancini in batches, without crowding, for 3–4 minutes. Drain on paper towels and leave for a couple of minutes before eating. Serve hot or at room temperature.

The risotto made for the arancini must be thick enough for the balls to hold their shape while they are being fried.

Ravida Estate in Menfi, Sicily.

PIZZA RUSTICA

THE NAME IS MISLEADING, BECAUSE PIZZA RUSTICA IS A PIE, NOT A PIZZA. THIS MEDIEVAL RECIPE IS UNUSUAL IN ITS COMBINATION OF A SWEET PASTRY CASE WITH A SAVOURY FILLING AND, LIKE MANY RICH PIES, PROBABLY BEGAN ITS LIFE AS A CELEBRATION DISH FOR COUNTRY FESTIVALS.

PASTRY
225 g plain flour
½ teaspoon baking powder
pinch of salt
100 g butter, chilled
55 g caster sugar
1 egg yolk
55 ml single cream

FILLING
500 g ricotta
3 eggs
50 g pecorino Romano, grated
100 g mozzarella, grated
125 g prosciutto, finely shredded
2 tablespoons finely chopped
  parsley

SERVES 6

TO MAKE the pastry, sift the flour, baking powder and salt into a large bowl. Cut the butter into cubes and add it to the bowl, then rub it in with your fingertips until the mixture resembles fine breadcrumbs. Stir in the sugar.

MIX the egg yolk and cream together and pour this into the pastry mixture. Mix together and then knead once or twice until you have a soft dough. Refrigerate until needed.

TO MAKE the filling, mix the ricotta with the eggs, cheese, prosciutto and parsley and season well with pepper—you probably won't need to add any salt if the prosciutto is salty. Preheat the oven to 200°C (400°F/Gas 6).

CUT one third off the pastry and roll out the remainder on a floured surface. Line a 20 x 4 cm pie tin and trim off any excess pastry. Fill the pastry case with the filling and smooth the top.

ROLL OUT the remaining pastry and cover the pie. Trim the edges and bake for 20 minutes, then reduce the temperature to 180°C (350°F/Gas 4) and bake for a further 20 minutes, or until the filling is cooked through.

A metal pie tin will give your pastry a good crisp finish and help it brown nicely on the outside. When putting in the filling, make sure you squash out any air bubbles so the pie is packed full.

SEAFOOD

LIGURIAN FISH STEW

THE FISH SUGGESTIONS BELOW ARE MERELY A GUIDELINE. TAKE YOUR FISHMONGER'S ADVICE ON WHAT IS FRESH AND SEASONAL. ASK FOR THE FISH TO BE PREPARED AND CUT INTO LARGE CHUNKS, THOUGH YOU WILL NEED THE BONES FOR YOUR STOCK (THIS CAN BE MADE IN ADVANCE AND FROZEN).

Skim the froth from the surface of the fish stock as it simmers.

Monkfish being skinned in the Vucciria market in Palermo.

FISH STOCK
250 g red mullet or red snapper fillet, cut into chunks, bones reserved
250 g cod, halibut or turbot fillet, cut into chunks, bones reserved
250 g monkfish fillet, or any other firm white fish, cut into chunks, bones reserved
6 large prawns or langoustines
1 small onion, roughly chopped
1 carrot, roughly chopped
15 g flat-leaf parsley, roughly chopped, stalks reserved

120 ml olive oil
1 red onion, halved and thinly sliced
1 large fennel bulb, thinly sliced
3 garlic cloves, thinly sliced
800 g tin tomatoes
300 ml dry white vermouth or wine
large pinch of saffron threads
450 g waxy potatoes, quartered lengthways
450 g mussels

SERVES 6

TO MAKE the fish stock, rinse the fish bones in cold water, removing any blood or intestines. Peel and devein the prawns and put the fish bones and prawn shells in a large saucepan with just enough water to cover. Bring slowly to a simmer, skimming any froth from the surface. Add the onion, carrot and the stalks from the parsley, then simmer gently for 20 minutes. Strain through a fine colander and measure 1 litre stock. If there is more than this, put the strained stock back into the saucepan and simmer until reduced to 1 litre.

TO MAKE the soup base, heat the olive oil in a large saucepan and cook the onion and fennel for about 5 minutes to soften. Add the garlic and tomatoes. Bring to the boil, then reduce the heat and simmer until the tomatoes have reduced to a thick sauce. Season and add 200 ml of the vermouth, the saffron and potatoes. Increase the heat and boil for about 5 minutes, then add the fish stock, reduce the heat and simmer for 10 minutes, or until the potatoes are cooked.

SCRUB the mussels, pull off the beards and discard any that are broken or cracked or don't close when tapped on the work surface. Bring 100 ml vermouth to the boil in another saucepan and add the mussels. Cover with a lid and cook quickly for about 1 minute, or until the shells have just opened (discard any that stay closed). Remove the mussels from their shells and place in a bowl. Pour over the remaining cooking liquid, discarding any sediment left in the pan.

ADD the prawns and fish to the soup. Stir briefly, season and simmer for 5 minutes, until the fish is cooked. Add the mussels at the last moment to reheat. Remove from the heat and leave for at least 10 minutes before serving. Add the parsley and serve in hot bowls with bread or crostini.

CALAMARI RIPIENI

IF YOUR FISHMONGER HAS HAD A CATCH OF SMALL TENDER SQUID, SNAP THEM UP—THIS IS THE PERFECT RECIPE FOR THEM. IF YOU ARE HAVING TO MAKE DO WITH LARGER SQUID, YOU MIGHT NEED TO INCREASE THE COOKING TIME AND TAKE CARE THAT THE LIQUID DOES NOT EVAPORATE.

TOMATO SAUCE
800 g tin tomatoes
100 ml red wine
2 tablespoons chopped flat-leaf
  parsley
pinch of sugar

STUFFING
600 g small squid
100 ml olive oil
1 small onion, finely chopped
1 small fennel bulb, finely chopped
2 garlic cloves, crushed
75 g risotto rice (arborio, vialone
  nano or carnaroli)
large pinch of saffron threads
1/2 large red chilli, chopped
150 ml white wine
2 tablespoons chopped flat-leaf
  parsley

SERVES 4

TO MAKE the sauce, put the tomatoes, red wine, parsley and sugar in a saucepan. Season and simmer until some of the liquid has evaporated.

TO MAKE the stuffing, prepare the squid by pulling the heads and tentacles out of the bodies with any innards. Cut the heads off below the eyes, just leaving the tentacles. Rinse the bodies, pulling out the transparent quills. Finely chop the tentacles and set aside with the squid bodies.

HEAT the oil in a saucepan, add the onion, fennel and garlic and cook gently for 10 minutes until soft. Add the rice, saffron, chilli and chopped tentacles and cook for a few minutes, stirring frequently until the tentacles are opaque. Season and add the white wine and 6 tablespoons of the tomato sauce. Cook, stirring frequently, until the tomato and wine has reduced into the rice. Add 150 ml water and continue cooking until the rice is tender and all the liquid has been absorbed. Add the parsley and cool for a few minutes.

STUFF the squid with the filling, using a teaspoon to push the filling down to the bottom of the squid sacks. Do not overfill—you need to close the tops of the sacks easily without any filling squeezing out. Seal the tops with cocktail sticks.

PUT the remaining tomato sauce in a saucepan with 200 ml water. Cook for 2 minutes, then add the stuffed squid, cover the pan and simmer gently for 30–45 minutes, depending on the size of the squid, until soft and tender. Don't stir, or the filling may fall out (if a little filling does fall out it will merely add flavour to the sauce). Shake the pan a little if you are worried about sticking.

REMOVE the cocktail sticks before serving, preferably with a salad and some bread.

Don't overfill the squid with stuffing or you'll find it leaking out into the tomato sauce.

Outdoor fish stall in Palermo, Sicily.

SARDINE RIPIENE

TO MAKE A SARDINE DISH MEMORABLE THE FISH MUST BE REALLY FRESH. SARDINES, LIKE MACKEREL, DO NOT LAST LONG OUT OF THE WATER SO DON'T ATTEMPT THIS RECIPE IF THE FISH LOOK TIRED. THIS RECIPE WILL SERVE TWO AS A MAIN COURSE OR FOUR AS AN ANTIPASTO.

8 medium-sized sardines, heads
   removed, scaled and gutted
4 tablespoons olive oil
1 small onion, thinly sliced
1 fennel bulb, thinly sliced
50 g pine nuts
4 tablespoons parsley,
   roughly chopped
15 g fresh breadcrumbs
1 large garlic clove, crushed
juice of 1/2 lemon
extra virgin olive oil
lemon wedges

SERVES 4

BUTTERFLY the sardines by pressing your fingers on either side of the backbone and gently easing it away from the flesh, following the line of the bone as you go. Remove the bone, leaving the tail attached to the flesh for a more attractive look. The fresher the fish, the harder this is to do, so you might want to ask your fishmonger to butterfly the sardines for you. (Alternatively, use fillets and put them back together to form a whole after cooking, although the result will not be as neat.) Rinse the fish in cold water and drain on paper towels. Leave in the fridge until needed.

PREHEAT the oven to 200°C (400°F/Gas 6). To prepare the stuffing, heat the olive oil in a frying pan and add the onion, fennel and pine nuts. Cook over moderately high heat until soft and light brown, stirring frequently. Mix 1 tablespoon of parsley with 1 tablespoon of breadcrumbs and set aside. Add the garlic and remaining breadcrumbs to the pan and cook for a few minutes more. Add the rest of the parsley, season and set aside. (This mixture can be made in advance and kept in the fridge, but bring back to room temperature before cooking.)

DRIZZLE a little olive oil in an ovenproof dish that will fit eight sardines in a single layer. Arrange the fish in the dish, skin side down, and season with salt and pepper. Spread the stuffing over the sardines and fold over to encase. (If you are using fillets, spread half with stuffing, then place the other fillets on top, skin side up, tail to tail like a sandwich.) Season again and sprinkle with the parsley and breadcrumb mixture. Drizzle with the lemon juice and a little extra virgin olive oil.

BAKE FOR 5–10 minutes, depending on the size of the sardines. (If the filling is still warm the sardines will cook faster.) Serve immediately or at room temperature with lemon wedges.

RED MULLET WITH FENNEL

2 fennel bulbs
2 tablespoons butter
2 tablespoons olive oil
1 onion, chopped
1 garlic clove, crushed
4 red mullet, gutted and scaled
extra virgin olive oil
1 lemon, quartered
2 teaspoons chopped oregano,
    or ¹/₂ teaspoon dried oregano
lemon wedges

SERVES 4

PREHEAT the oven to 190°C (375°F/Gas 5) and grease a large shallow ovenproof dish. Finely slice the fennel, keeping the green fronds.

HEAT the butter and olive oil in a large frying pan and gently cook the fennel, onion and garlic for 12–15 minutes until softened but not browned. Season with salt and pepper.

STUFF EACH fish with a heaped tablespoon of the fennel mixture and a quarter of the fennel fronds. Brush with extra virgin olive oil, squeeze a lemon quarter over each one and season well.

SPOON the remainder of the cooked fennel into the dish and sprinkle with half of the oregano. Arrange the fish, side by side, on top. Sprinkle the remaining oregano over the fish and cover the dish loosely with foil. Bake for 25 minutes, or until just cooked through. Serve with lemon wedges.

Brushing the fish with oil prevents the skin from drying out while it bakes and helps the seasoning to stick to the fish skin.

BAKED SWORDFISH SICILIANA

FISHED MAINLY OFF THE COAST OF SICILY, SWORDFISH HAS A FIRM MEATY TEXTURE. WHILE MANY MORE DELICATE FISH WOULD BE OVERPOWERED BY THE STRONG MEDITERRANEAN FLAVOURS OF THIS DISH, THE MORE ROBUST FLESH OF THE SWORDFISH CAN HOLD ITS OWN. YOU CAN ALSO USE TUNA.

80 ml olive oil
2 tablespoons lemon juice
2¹/₂ tablespoons finely chopped
    basil
4 swordfish steaks
60 g pitted black olives, chopped
1 tablespoon baby capers
¹/₂ teaspoon finely chopped
    anchovies in olive oil
400 g tomatoes, peeled, seeded
    and chopped
2 tablespoons dried breadcrumbs

SERVES 4

MIX half the olive oil with the lemon juice and 1 tablespoon of the basil. Season and pour into a shallow ovenproof dish, large enough to hold the swordfish in a single layer. Arrange the swordfish in the dish and leave to marinate for 15 minutes, turning once. Preheat the oven to 230°C (450°F/Gas 8) and preheat the grill.

COMBINE the olives, capers, anchovies and tomatoes with the remaining olive oil and basil and season well. Spread over the swordfish and sprinkle the breadcrumbs over the top. Bake for about 20 minutes, or until the fish is just opaque. Finish off by placing briefly under the hot grill until the breadcrumbs are crisp. Serve with bread to soak up the juices.

BAKED SWORDFISH SICILIANA

Cod from Northern Europe was traditionally preserved in salt for consumption inland. Its popularity in Mediterranean countries is a legacy of meatless 'humility' days observed by the Catholic church.

SALT COD FRITTERS

225 g salt cod
1 small onion, sliced
2 garlic cloves, sliced
1 bay leaf
400 ml milk
100 ml dry white vermouth or white wine
200 g potatoes, chopped
2 tablespoons flat-leaf parsley, roughly chopped
pinch of nutmeg
1 egg yolk
1 tablespoon plain flour, plus a little extra for dusting
500 ml oil for frying

SERVES 4

SOAK the salt cod in cold water for 24 hours, changing the water about four times.

PUT the onion, garlic, bay leaf, milk and vermouth in a saucepan, season with pepper and bring to the boil. Add the salt cod, reduce the heat and simmer, covered, for 10–15 minutes until the fish is cooked and flakes away from the skin. Leave in the liquid until cool enough to handle. Meanwhile, boil the potatoes until tender, then drain and cool.

PLACE the fish on a board and flake the flesh away from the skin and bones. Put the flaked fish in a bowl and add the potato, parsley, nutmeg, egg yolk, flour and a little pepper. Mix well and taste for seasoning—you should not need to add any more salt. Leave in the fridge for 15 minutes and then roll into small balls and flatten slightly.

HEAT the oil in a frying pan. Dust the fritters with flour and fry in batches in the hot oil for about 2 minutes on each side. Drain on paper towels and serve warm, perhaps with a tomato sauce.

TUNA WITH BEANS

400 g dried beans, such as cannellini
1 bay leaf
1 garlic clove
150 ml olive oil
1 small red onion, finely sliced
2 tablespoons finely chopped parsley
400 g tin tuna in olive oil, drained

SERVES 4

SOAK the beans overnight in plenty of cold water. Rinse them and transfer to a very large saucepan. Cover with plenty of cold water and bring to the boil. Add the bay leaf, garlic and 1 tablespoon olive oil, cover and simmer for 1–1½ hours or until tender, depending on the age of the beans. Salt the water for the last 15–20 minutes of cooking. The beans should keep their shape and have a slight bite rather than being soft.

DRAIN WELL, remove the bay leaf and garlic and transfer the beans to a shallow serving dish. Add the onion and remaining olive oil and season with salt and pepper. Toss well, then chill.

TOSS through two-thirds of the parsley and taste for seasoning. Break the tuna up into bite-sized pieces and toss through the beans. Sprinkle the remaining parsley over the top and serve.

TUNA WITH BEANS

84

CHARGRILLED SHELLFISH

THIS RECIPE CALLS FOR DUBLIN BAY PRAWNS BUT, IF YOU CAN'T FIND THEM, ANY PRAWNS WILL DO. USING A ROSEMARY TWIG FOR BASTING GIVES THE MARINADE A SUBTLE HERB FLAVOUR, WITHOUT ALLOWING IT TO BECOME OVERPOWERING.

125 ml extra virgin olive oil
2 garlic cloves
1 tablespoon finely chopped basil
80 ml lemon juice
12 Dublin Bay prawns (scampi or
    gamberoni)
12 scallops in the half shell
16 prawns
long sturdy rosemary twig, for
    basting
16 large clams (sea dates, warty
    venus shells, pipis or vongole)

SERVES 4

COMBINE the oil, garlic cloves, basil and lemon juice in a bowl and season well. Set aside to infuse for 15–20 minutes.

REMOVE the claws and heads from the Dublin Bay prawns, then butterfly by splitting them down the underside with a sharp knife and opening them out.

REMOVE the scallops from their shells, reserving the shells, and pull away the white muscle and digestive tract around each one, leaving the roes intact if you like. Peel and devein the prawns, leaving the tails intact.

PREHEAT a griddle or barbecue until hot. Using the rosemary twig as a brush, lightly brush the cut surfaces of the Dublin Bay prawns with the oil dressing. Brush the griddle or barbecue plate with the dressing (be careful of the flame flaring) and place the Dublin Bay prawns on to cook, shell sides down.

AFTER 30 seconds, brush the scallops with the dressing and add them to the griddle with the prawns and clams (discard any clams that are broken or don't close when tapped). Turn the Dublin Bay prawns over and cook for another minute. Turn the prawns once. Baste with more dressing once or twice. All the shellfish should be ready within 3–4 minutes—the clams can be moved to the side and brushed with a little dressing as they open. Put the scallops back on their shells.

DISCARD the garlic cloves and pour the oil dressing into a small serving bowl. Transfer the shellfish to a warm serving platter. Serve at once with the dressing, bread and finger bowls.

Dublin Bay prawns have more meat than many other prawns. Butterflying allows the flesh to cook through the shell and take on the flavour of the rosemary.

STUFFED MUSSELS

MUSSELS ARE ESPECIALLY POPULAR IN THE PUGLIA REGION—THE HEEL OF ITALY'S 'BOOT'. THIS DISH, FLAVOURED WITH OLIVE OIL, GARLIC, TOMATO AND BASIL, EPITOMISES THE FLAVOURS OF THAT STRETCH OF MEDITERRANEAN COAST.

24 mussels
3 tablespoons olive oil
4 garlic cloves, crushed
500 ml tomato passata
1½ tablespoons roughly chopped
  basil
15 g parsley, finely chopped
40 g fresh white breadcrumbs
2 eggs, beaten
pinch of cayenne pepper

SERVES 4

CLEAN the mussels by scrubbing them thoroughly. Discard any that are broken or cracked or do not close when tapped on the work surface. Insert a sharp knife at the point where the beard protrudes and prise the shell open, leaving the mussel intact inside and keeping the two shells attached. Pull out the beard and discard. Rinse the mussels.

HEAT the oil in a large saucepan and gently cook half the garlic for 15–20 seconds, without browning. Add the passata and basil, season lightly with salt and pepper and bring to the boil. Reduce the heat and simmer for 5 minutes, then add 300 ml cold water. Return to the boil, cover and keep at a low simmer until needed.

COMBINE the parsley, breadcrumbs and the remaining garlic, then blend in the eggs. Add the cayenne pepper and season. Using a teaspoon, fill each mussel with a little of this mixture. Tie the mussels closed with kitchen string as you go, to prevent the filling escaping.

WHEN the mussels have all been stuffed, place them in the tomato sauce and simmer, covered, for 10 minutes.

LIFT OUT the mussels with a slotted spoon and remove the string. Pile on a warm platter and serve with the tomato sauce, bread and finger bowls.

The stuffing of parsley, breadcrumbs and garlic is bound together with beaten egg. The mussels are filled with the stuffing and tied with lengths of kitchen string, then simmered in tomato sauce. Remove the string before you serve.

ROAST EEL WITH BAY LEAVES

2 x 800 g eels or 1 x 1.25 kg eel,
   skinned
2 lemons, halved
4 garlic cloves
25–30 large bay leaves (not dried)
coarse sea salt

SERVES 4

PREHEAT the oven to 200°C (400°F/Gas 6).
Lightly brush a large shallow casserole with oil.
Rub the eel with a cloth to wipe off some of the
shine, then rub it with the cut side of half a lemon.
Cut the eel into 5 cm sections, discarding the
head and the section behind it that contains
the gut.

ARRANGE HALF the eel pieces in a single layer in
the casserole. Scatter with the garlic cloves and
squeeze some lemon juice over the top. Sprinkle
lightly with pepper. Scatter half the bay leaves
over the top, then liberally sprinkle with salt.
Repeat the layers with the remaining ingredients.
Bake for 35–40 minutes, or until the eel is tender.

ROAST EEL WITH BAY LEAVES

GRILLED MACKEREL

4 small mackerel, cleaned
4 tablespoons olive oil
2 garlic cloves, roughly chopped
1/2 teaspoon paprika
1 tablespoon lemon juice
8 small rosemary sprigs, plus
   4 more to serve
lemon wedges

SERVES 4

BUTTERFLY the mackerel by pressing your fingers
on either side of the backbone and gently easing
it away from the flesh, following the line of the
bone as you go. Remove the bone, leaving the tail
attached to the flesh for a more attractive look.

COMBINE the olive oil, garlic, paprika and lemon
juice in a shallow bowl large enough to take the
mackerel side by side. Season well. Make two
diagonal cuts on each side of the fish and leave in
the marinade for 30 minutes, turning once.

PREHEAT a griddle or barbecue. Brush the garlic
from the fish. Secure a rosemary sprig on each
side of the mackerel with wooden toothpicks or, if
using a barbecue, use four small metal fish grilling
frames (the rosemary will be kept in place by the
frame, and the fish can be turned easily).

BRUSH the grill with olive oil, adjust the heat to
moderate and add the mackerel. Grill, turning
once, for 5 minutes each side or until they are
cooked through. Gently remove the rosemary.
Serve each fish with a wedge of lemon and
garnish with a fresh sprig of rosemary.

Leave the heads on the mackerel
if you prefer to serve whole fish.

GRILLED MACKEREL

POULTRY, MEAT & GAME

Early morning shopping in Bologna.

CHICKEN CACCIATORA

JUST LIKE THE FRENCH *CHASSEUR*, CACCIATORA MEANS 'HUNTER'S STYLE'. THE DISH IS ORIGINALLY FROM CENTRAL ITALY, BUT LIKE SO MUCH ITALIAN FARE, EVERY REGION HAS PUT ITS OWN TWIST ON THE RECIPE. THIS ONE, WITH TOMATOES, IS PROBABLY THE MOST WIDELY TRAVELLED.

3 tablespoons olive oil
1 large onion, finely chopped
3 garlic cloves, crushed
1 stalk celery, finely chopped
150 g pancetta, finely chopped
125 g button mushrooms, thickly sliced
4 chicken drumsticks
4 chicken thighs
90 ml dry vermouth or dry white wine
2 x 400 g tins chopped tomatoes
1/4 teaspoon brown sugar
1 oregano sprig, plus 4–5 sprigs to garnish
1 rosemary sprig
1 bay leaf

SERVES 4

HEAT half the oil in a large casserole. Add the onion, garlic and celery and cook, stirring from time to time, over moderately low heat for 6–8 minutes until the onion is golden.

ADD the pancetta and mushrooms, increase the heat and cook, stirring occasionally, for 4–5 minutes. Spoon out onto a plate and set aside.

ADD the remaining olive oil to the casserole and lightly brown the chicken pieces, a few at a time. Season them as they brown. Spoon off any excess fat and return all the pieces to the casserole. Add the vermouth, increase the heat and cook until the liquid has almost evaporated.

ADD the tomatoes, sugar, oregano, rosemary, bay leaf and 75 ml cold water. Bring to the boil then stir in the reserved pancetta mixture. Cover and leave to simmer for 20 minutes, or until the chicken is tender but not falling off the bone.

IF the liquid is too thin, remove the chicken from the casserole, increase the heat and boil until thickened. Discard the sprigs of herbs and taste for salt and pepper. Toss in the additional oregano sprigs and the dish is ready to serve.

POLLO ALLA DIAVOLA

DEVIL'S CHICKEN ORIGINATED IN THE TUSCAN KITCHEN. THE CHICKEN IS BUTTERFLIED, THEN MARINATED IN OLIVE OIL AND CHILLI. TRADITIONALLY THE BIRD WOULD BE COOKED ON A GRILL OVER AN OPEN FIRE—THE FLAMES LICKING UP FROM BELOW LIKE THE FIRES OF THE DEVIL.

2 x 900 g chickens
150 ml olive oil
juice of 1 large lemon
2 sage leaves
3–4 very small red chillies, finely
    minced, or $^{1}/_{2}$ teaspoon dried
    chilli flakes
2 shallots
2 garlic cloves
4 tablespoons chopped parsley
$2^{1}/_{2}$ tablespoons softened butter
lemon slices

SERVES 4

SPLIT EACH chicken through the breastbone and press open to form a butterfly, joined down the back. Flatten with your hand to give a uniform surface for cooking. Place in a shallow dish large enough to take both chickens side by side.

MIX TOGETHER the olive oil, lemon juice, sage and chilli in a bowl and season well with salt and pepper. Pour over the chicken and leave to marinate in the fridge for 30 minutes. Turn the chickens and leave for a further 30 minutes.

MEANWHILE, chop the shallots, garlic, parsley and butter in a blender or food processor until fine and paste-like. (If you want to do this by hand, chop the vegetables and then mix them into the softened butter.) Season with salt and pepper. Preheat the grill.

PLACE the chickens, skin side down, on a grill tray. Position about 10 cm below the heat and grill for 10 minutes, basting with the marinade once or twice. Turn the chickens and grill, basting occasionally, for another 10–12 minutes, or until the juices run clear when a thigh is pierced deeply with a skewer.

SPREAD the butter paste over the skin of the chickens with a knife. Reduce the heat and grill for about 3 minutes until the coating is lightly browned. Serve hot or cold, with lemon wedges.

Wild chillies have been eaten in Mexico since 7000 BC. It is likely that the plants were brought to Europe by Columbus—the chilli reached southern Italy in 1526 and, as in many other countries, was absorbed into local dishes.

Monti Sibillini, Umbria

ROAST CHICKEN WITH ROSEMARY

TURNING THE CHICKEN REGULARLY DURING ROASTING KEEPS THE BREAST MEAT BEAUTIFULLY MOIST—THE JUICES RUN INTO IT INSTEAD OF DRAINING AWAY INTO THE TIN. THE REGULAR TURNING ALSO KEEPS THE BIRD FROM FLATTENING ON ANY ONE SIDE.

2 rosemary sprigs
3 garlic cloves
1 teaspoon balsamic vinegar
1 x 1.5 kg chicken
2 tablespoons extra virgin olive oil
2 tablespoons olive oil
125 ml chicken stock

SERVES 4

PREHEAT the oven to 200°C (400°F/Gas 6). Put one rosemary sprig, the garlic and balsamic vinegar inside the cavity of the chicken. Add a large pinch of salt and a few grinds of black pepper. Truss the legs together.

RUB the extra virgin olive oil over the chicken skin. Pour the olive oil into a roasting tin and put the chicken in the tin, breast up. Place the second sprig of rosemary on top.

TRANSFER TO the oven and roast for 1 hour, turning the chicken and basting with the pan juices every 15 minutes.

PUT the chicken on a warm serving plate and discard the rosemary sprig. Spoon off the fat from the roasting tin and place it over high heat on the stovetop. Add the chicken stock and deglaze the pan. Boil until reduced and thickened. Taste for salt and pepper, then pour into a sauceboat to accompany the chicken. Serve with roast rosemary potatoes.

Markets in Italy are usually held in a special square known as the *Piazza Erbe*.

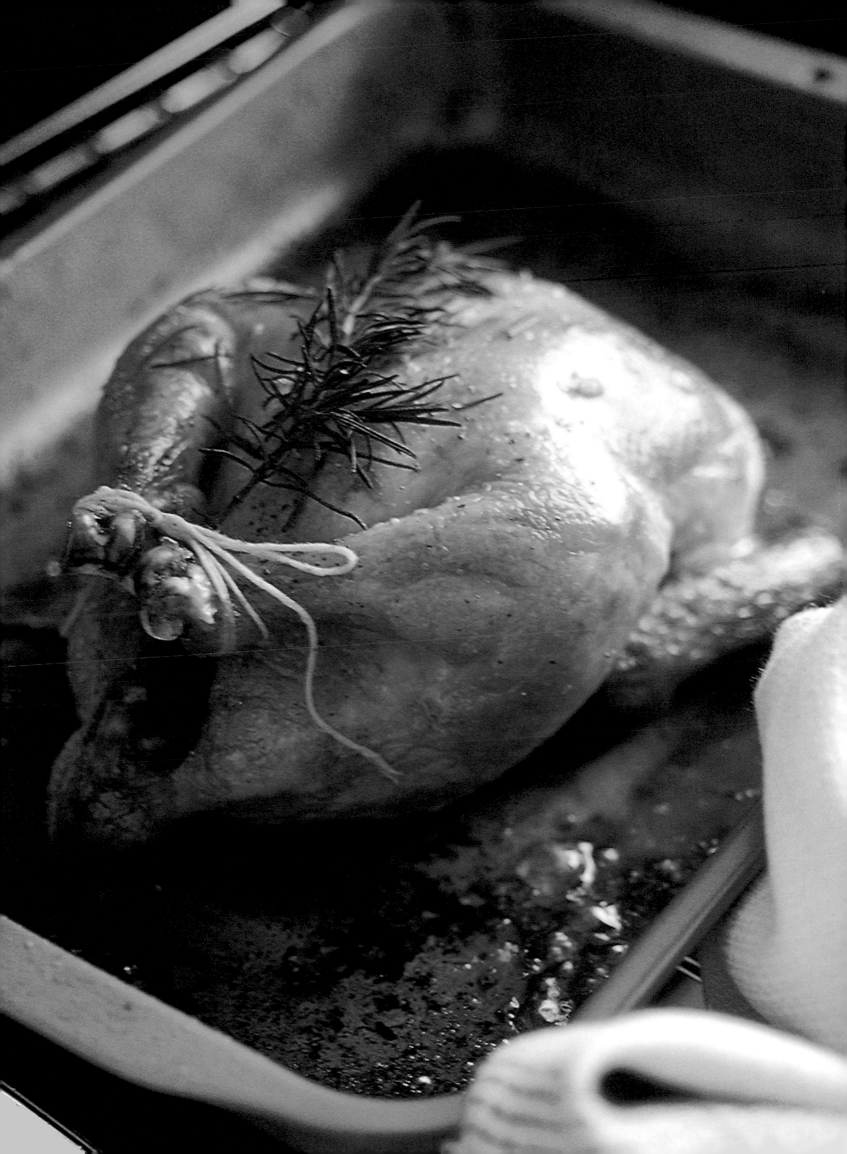

VINEGAR-POACHED CHICKEN

LIKE A LOT OF ITALIAN FOOD, THE SIMPLICITY OF THIS DISH MEANS YOU REALLY DO NEED TO USE THE BEST-QUALITY INGREDIENTS. BUY A FREE-RANGE BIRD—YOU'LL FIND IT HAS A GREAT DEAL MORE FLAVOUR FOR JUST A LITTLE MORE EXPENSE. USE ANY LEFTOVER POACHING LIQUID FOR SOUP STOCK.

4 x 500 g small chickens or
    poussin
1 large carrot, chopped
1 large onion, chopped
1 celery stalk, chopped
bouquet garni
1¹/₂ tablespoons sugar
500 ml white wine vinegar
3 tablespoons balsamic vinegar
1 tablespoon butter
1 tablespoon plain flour
150 ml chicken stock
4 rosemary sprigs

SERVES 4

The chickens are simmered in liquid to keep the flesh moist and infuse it with the vinegar flavour.

TRIM ANY fat from the chickens and season well with salt and pepper, both inside and out. Tie the legs together and tuck the wings behind the chicken. Spread out the carrot, onion and celery in a casserole large enough to take the chickens side by side (don't add the chickens yet, though). Add the bouquet garni, sugar, white wine vinegar and balsamic vinegar and bring to the boil. Reduce the heat and simmer for 5 minutes.

PLACE the chickens on top of the vegetables, breast up. Add enough boiling water to cover the birds, put the lid on the casserole and simmer for 25 minutes, or until they are just cooked. Turn off the heat and leave the chickens in the casserole for 10 minutes.

MELT the butter in a small saucepan. Add the flour and cook, stirring, for 30 seconds. Gradually stir in the chicken stock and simmer until smooth and thickened. Stir in 3–4 tablespoons of the chicken poaching liquid and then taste. Continue adding a little poaching liquid (probably about 125 ml in total) until the sauce is to your taste. Increase the heat and boil until slightly thickened. Season with salt and pepper.

REMOVE the chickens from the casserole, drain well and arrange on a warm serving platter. Spoon just enough sauce over the chickens to glaze the skin, garnish with the rosemary sprigs and serve.

The home of balsamic vinegar is Modena, where authentic vinegars aged for at least 12 years (usually much more) are labelled *aceto balsamico tradizionale di Modena*. Originally made only by wealthy families who could afford to wait for their vinegar to mature, a version is now produced commercially and sold without the *'tradizionale'* label.

Blanch fresh vine leaves in boiling water before use.

QUAILS WRAPPED IN VINE LEAVES

4 rosemary sprigs
4 quails
2 tablespoons olive oil
4 teaspoons balsamic vinegar
2 teaspoons brown sugar
4 large vine leaves

SERVES 4

PREHEAT the oven to 180°C (350°F/Gas 4). Stuff a sprig of rosemary into each quail and then tie its legs together. Tuck the wings behind the back.

HEAT the olive oil in a frying pan and add the quails. Brown them all over and then add the vinegar and sugar and bubble everything together. Remove from the heat.

BLANCH the vine leaves in boiling water for 15 seconds and then wrap one around each quail. Put the wrapped quail in a roasting tin, seam side down, and bake for 15 minutes.

GRILLED QUAILS

QUAILS REALLY ARE BEST COOKED SIMPLY AND WITHOUT MUCH FUSS. IN THIS RECIPE THE TINY BIRDS ARE JUST MARINATED AND GRILLED. THE COOKING TIME IS SHORT, BUT THE GOLDEN RULE WITH QUAILS IS NOT TO OVERCOOK THEM. THE RECIPE ALSO WORKS WELL WITH PIGEON.

Marinating the quail with lemon juice and olive oil.

4 quails
2$\frac{1}{2}$ tablespoons lemon juice
4 tablespoons olive oil
8 small sage leaves
2 garlic cloves, halved
1 small red chilli, seeded and
    roughly chopped
2 tablespoons chopped parsley
lemon wedges

SERVES 4

SPLIT EACH quail through the breastbone with a sharp knife and then turn it over. Press open hard with the heel of your hand to form a spatchcock. Transfer the quails to a shallow dish large enough to hold all the birds side by side.

MIX TOGETHER the lemon juice, olive oil, sage leaves, garlic and chilli, and season to taste with salt and pepper. Pour over the quails and leave to marinate for 30 minutes, turning the birds after 15 minutes. Preheat the grill.

PLACE the quails, skin side up, on a grill tray. Position them 12–15 cm below the heat and grill for about 5 minutes on each side, or until golden and cooked through.

SERVE hot or cold, with a sprinkling of chopped parsley and lemon wedges.

GRILLED QUAILS

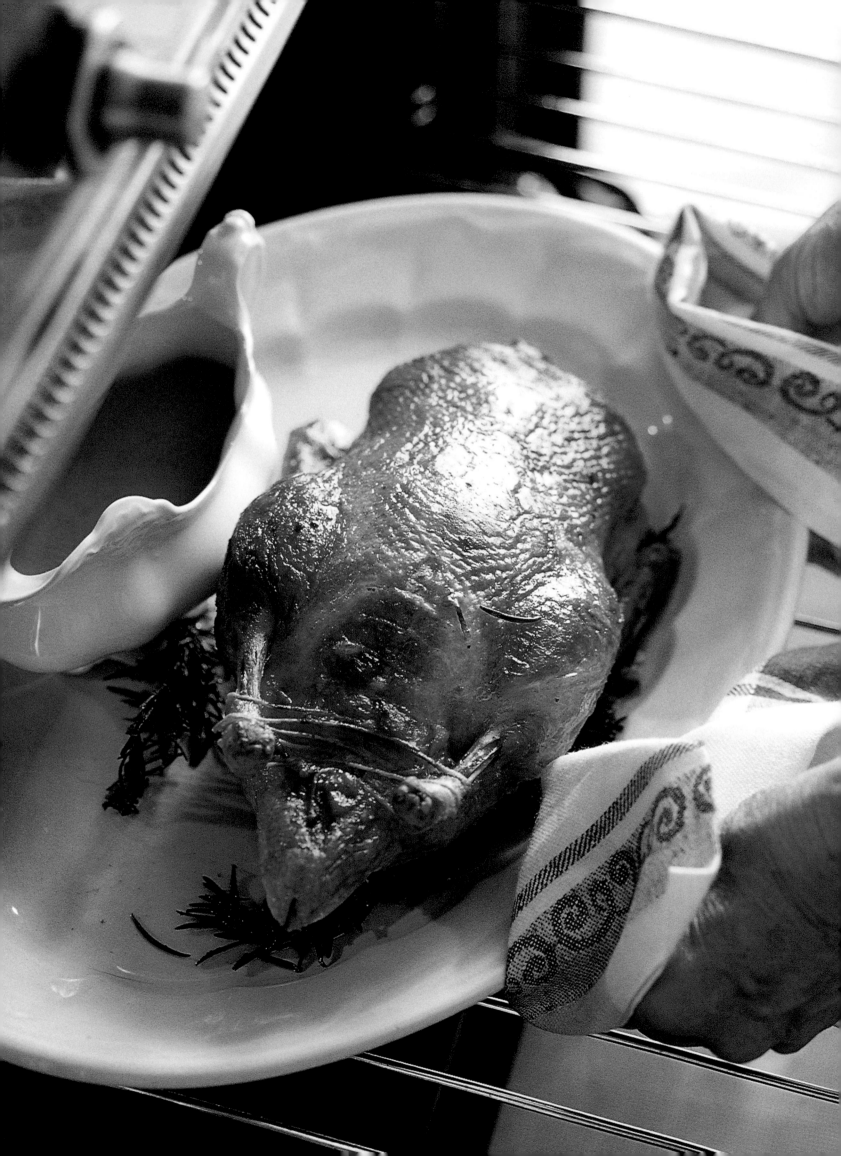

ROAST DUCK WITH PARMA HAM

PARMA HAM WAS SUPPOSEDLY SERVED TO HANNIBAL AT A BANQUET IN THE CITY IN 217 BC. TODAY ITS PRODUCTION IS A LICENSED INDUSTRY, WITH ONLY HAM FROM THE EMILIA-ROMAGNA REGION TAKING THE NAME. THESE HAMS HAVE THE DUCAL CROWN OF PARMA BRANDED ON THEIR SKIN.

2 thick slices 'country-style' bread, such as ciabatta, crusts removed
125 ml milk
1 x 2 kg duck
6 thick slices Parma ham
3 garlic cloves, crushed
120 g minced pork
120 g minced veal
2 shallots, finely chopped
2 tablespoons grated Parmesan
1 tablespoon finely chopped parsley
1 egg
75 ml olive oil
60 g lard or butter
2 rosemary sprigs
4 tablespoons grappa or brandy
250 ml chicken stock
3 tablespoons double cream

SERVES 4

PREHEAT the oven to 220°C (425°F/Gas 7). Soak the bread in the milk. Remove any excess skin and fat from the duck, leaving just enough skin to sew the cavity closed later.

BRING a large saucepan of water to the boil. Prick the skin of the duck all over and put it into the boiling water with a teaspoon of salt. Boil for 12 minutes. Remove and place, cavity side down, in a colander to drain for 10 minutes. Dry well all over, inside and out, with paper towels.

FINELY CHOP 2 slices of Parma ham and mix with the garlic, minced pork and veal, shallots, Parmesan and parsley. Squeeze the bread dry and add to the mixture. Add the egg, season and mix well. Fill the duck cavity with the stuffing then stitch closed with kitchen string. Tie the wings and legs together with string.

PUT the olive oil, lard and rosemary in a roasting tin and heat in the oven for 5 minutes. Put the duck in the middle, breast up, and roast for 10 minutes. Baste with the pan juices and lay the remaining slices of Parma ham over the breast, covering the legs as well. Reduce the temperature to 190°C (375°F/Gas 5) and roast for a further hour, basting several times. Remove the Parma ham, increase the heat to 210°C (415°F/Gas 6–7) and return to the oven for 10 minutes.

TRANSFER the duck to a carving plate and leave to rest for 10 minutes. Spoon all the fat out of the roasting tin, leaving just the duck juices, and place the tin over high heat on the stove. Add the grappa and cook until it is syrupy and almost evaporated, then add the chicken stock. Continue boiling until slightly thickened, then add the cream. Season well and strain into a sauceboat. Remove the string, carve the duck and stir any juices into the sauce before serving.

Stuff the duck, then stitch up the opening with kitchen string—you can buy special large needles from kitchen shops. The slices of ham prevent the duck drying out.

Pistachios ripen on a tree in Sicily.

Marsala is a fortified wine that takes its name from the town in Sicily where the grapes are grown. It was created by an English wine shipper in 1773, who added grape spirit to wine to prevent it spoiling at sea.

ROAST TURKEY WITH PISTACHIO STUFFING

ITALIAN ROAST TURKEY IS TRADITIONALLY SERVED WITH *MOSTARDA DI CREMONA*, A TYPE OF ITALIAN CHUTNEY, MADE FROM CANDIED FRUIT SUCH AS PEAR, APRICOT, MELON AND ORANGE PRESERVED WITH MUSTARD, HONEY, WINE AND SPICES. YOU CAN ALSO USE THIS RECIPE TO ROAST GUINEA FOWL.

STUFFING
45 g shelled pistachio nuts
100 g prosciutto, finely chopped
220 g minced pork
220 g minced chicken
1 egg
90 ml double cream
150 g chestnut purée
1/2 teaspoon finely chopped sage or
    1/4 teaspoon dried sage
pinch of cayenne pepper

1 x 3 kg turkey
300 g butter, softened
1 onion, roughly chopped
4 sage leaves
1 rosemary sprig
1/2 celery stalk, cut into 2–3 pieces
1 carrot, cut into 3–4 pieces
250 ml dry white wine
125 ml dry Marsala
250 ml chicken stock

SERVES 8

TO MAKE the stuffing, preheat the oven to 170°C (325°F/Gas 3). Spread the pistachio nuts on a baking tray and toast for 6–8 minutes. Place in a bowl with the other stuffing ingredients, season well and mix together thoroughly.

FILL the turkey cavity with the stuffing and sew up the opening with kitchen string. Cross the legs and tie them together, and tuck the wings behind the body. Rub the skin with 100 g of the butter. Put the onion in the centre of a roasting tin and place the turkey on top, breast up. Add another 100 g of butter to the tin with the sage, rosemary, celery and carrot. Pour the white wine and Marsala over the top. Roast for 2 1/2–3 hours, basting several times. Cover with buttered greaseproof paper when the skin becomes golden brown.

TRANSFER the turkey to a carving plate and leave to rest in a warm spot. Put the vegetables from the pan into a food processor and blend, or push them through a sieve. Add the pan juices and scrapings from the bottom of the tin and blend until smooth. Transfer the mixture to a saucepan, add the remaining 100 g of butter and the chicken stock and bring to the boil. Season and cook until thickened to a good gravy consistency. Transfer to a gravy boat.

CARVE the turkey and serve with stuffing and gravy, and preferably *mostarda di Cremona*.

VENISON CASSEROLE

A DARK GAMEY MEAT LIKE VENISON NEEDS STRONG FLAVOURS TO BALANCE IT. THIS CASSEROLE
CONTAINS CLOVES, JUNIPER AND ALLSPICE—ALL ROBUST FLAVOURINGS IN THEIR OWN RIGHT. SERVE
WITH CREAMY POLENTA OR POTATOES TO MOP UP THE RICH GRAVY.

1 rosemary sprig
1 large onion
1 garlic clove
80 g prosciutto
100 g butter
1 kg venison, cut into large cubes
1 litre beef stock
75 ml red wine vinegar
100 ml robust red wine
2 cloves
4 juniper berries
pinch of allspice
1 bay leaf
3 tablespoons plain flour
2 tablespoons dry Marsala or
   brandy
1¹/₂ teaspoons grated lemon zest
1¹/₂ tablespoons finely chopped
   parsley

SERVES 4

STRIP the leaves off the rosemary and chop them
finely with the onion, garlic and prosciutto. Heat
half the butter in a large heavy saucepan with a
lid. Add the chopped mixture and soften over
moderately low heat for 5 minutes. Season with
pepper. Increase the heat, add the venison and
cook for 10 minutes, or until brown on all sides.

PUT the stock in another saucepan and bring
to the boil, then reduce the heat and keep at a
low simmer.

INCREASE the heat under the venison, add the
vinegar and cook until the liquid becomes thick
and syrupy. Pour in the red wine. When that
becomes syrupy, stir in half of the simmering
stock. Add the cloves, juniper berries, allspice and
bay leaf and cover the pan. Simmer for 1 hour,
stirring once or twice and adding a little hot water
if necessary to maintain the liquid level.

MEANWHILE, melt the remaining butter in a
saucepan. Stir in the flour and cook over
moderately low heat for 1 minute. Slowly stir in
the remaining stock and cook until the sauce
thickens slightly.

STIR the sauce into the venison casserole, then
add the Marsala. Uncover the pan and simmer for
a further 20 minutes. Taste for salt and pepper.
Mix together the lemon zest and parsley and
sprinkle over the top before serving.

La Kalsa, Palermo.

VEAL SALTIMBOCCA

8 small veal escalopes
8 slices prosciutto
8 sage leaves
2 tablespoons olive oil
60 g butter
185 ml dry white wine or dry
   Marsala

SERVES 4

PLACE the veal between two sheets of clingfilm and pound with a meat mallet until an even thickness. Season lightly. Cut the prosciutto slices to the same size as the veal. Cover each piece of veal with a slice of prosciutto and place a sage leaf on top. Secure in place with a cocktail stick.

HEAT the oil and half the butter in a large frying pan. Add the veal in batches and fry, prosciutto up, over moderately high heat for 3–4 minutes, or until the veal is just cooked through. Transfer each batch to a hot plate as it is done.

POUR OFF the oil from the pan and add the wine. Cook over high heat until reduced by half, scraping up the bits from the bottom of the pan. Add the remaining butter and, when it has melted, season. Spoon over the veal to serve.

The cocktail stick will hold together the sage, prosciutto and veal. Take it out just before serving.

VEAL ALLA MILANESE

8 veal chops
2 eggs
60 g fine dried breadcrumbs
3 tablespoons grated Parmesan
3 tablespoons butter
1 tablespoon oil
4 lemon wedges dipped in finely
   chopped parsley

SERVES 4

CUT ALL the fat from the veal chops and trim the lower rib bone until it is clean of all fat and flesh. Place each chop between two sheets of clingfilm and pound the flesh with a meat mallet until it is half its original thickness.

LIGHTLY BEAT the eggs with salt and pepper and pour into a dish. Combine the breadcrumbs and Parmesan and place in another dish. Dip each chop into the egg, coating it on both sides. Shake off the excess egg, then coat the chop with the breadcrumb mix, pressing each side firmly into the crumbs. Place all the chops on a plate and chill for 30 minutes.

HEAT the butter and oil in a large frying pan. As soon as the butter stops foaming, add the chops and fry gently for 4 minutes on each side, until the breadcrumbs are deep golden. Serve immediately with the lemon wedges.

VEAL ALLA MILANESE

OSSO BUCO ALLA MILANESE

OSSO BUCO IS A MILANESE DISH AND TRADITIONALLY TOMATOES ARE NOT USED IN THE COOKING OF NORTHERN ITALY. THE ABSENCE OF THE ROBUST TOMATO ALLOWS THE MORE DELICATE FLAVOUR OF THE GREMOLATA TO FEATURE IN THIS CLASSIC OSSO BUCO. SERVE WITH *RISOTTO ALLA MILANESE*.

12 pieces veal shank, about 4 cm
   thick
plain flour, seasoned with salt and
   pepper
60 ml olive oil
60 g butter
1 garlic clove
250 ml dry white wine
1 bay leaf or lemon leaf
pinch of allspice
pinch of ground cinnamon

GREMOLATA
2 teaspoons grated lemon rind
6 tablespoons finely chopped
   parsley
1 garlic clove, finely chopped

thin lemon wedges

SERVES 4

TIE EACH piece of veal shank around its girth to secure the flesh, then dust with the seasoned flour. Heat the oil, butter and garlic in a large heavy saucepan big enough to hold the shanks in a single layer. Put the shanks in the pan and cook for 12–15 minutes until well browned. Arrange the shanks, standing them up in a single layer, pour in the wine and add the bay leaf, allspice and cinnamon. Cover the saucepan.

COOK AT a low simmer for 15 minutes, then add 125 ml warm water. Continue cooking, covered, for about 45 minutes to 1 hour (the timing will depend on the age of the veal) until the meat is tender and you can cut it with a fork. Check the volume of liquid once or twice and add more warm water as needed. Transfer the veal to a plate and keep warm. Discard the garlic clove and bay leaf.

TO MAKE the gremolata, mix together the lemon rind, parsley and garlic. Increase the heat under the saucepan and stir for 1–2 minutes until the sauce is thick, scraping up any bits off the bottom of the saucepan as you stir. Stir in the gremolata. Season with salt and pepper if necessary and return the veal to the sauce. Heat through, then serve with the lemon wedges.

The pan for osso buco must be large enough to fit the shank pieces in a single layer so that they cook through evenly.

Ask your butcher to cut the osso buco from the hind shin of the veal where the meat is more tender. The pieces should have a high proportion of meat to bone.

Tying herbs together as a bouquet garni means they are much easier to lift out when the dish is cooked.

OSSO BUCO WITH TOMATOES

THIS IS THE OSSO BUCO WITH WHICH MANY OF US ARE FAMILIAR. THE TOMATO-BASED VERSION MAY NOT BE COMPLETELY AUTHENTIC, BUT ITS ENDURING POPULARITY VOUCHES FOR ITS FLAVOUR. SERVE WITH CREAMY POLENTA TO CATCH THE JUICES.

10 pieces veal shank, about 4 cm thick
plain flour, seasoned with salt and pepper
60 ml olive oil
60 g butter
1 garlic clove
1 small carrot, finely chopped
1 large onion, finely chopped
1/2 celery stalk, finely chopped
250 ml dry white wine
375 ml veal or chicken stock
400 g tin chopped tomatoes
bouquet garni

SERVES 4

TIE EACH piece of veal shank around its girth to secure the flesh, then dust with the seasoned flour. Heat the oil, butter and garlic in a large heavy saucepan big enough to hold the shanks in a single layer. Put the shanks in the saucepan and cook for 12–15 minutes until well browned. Remove the shanks from the saucepan and set aside. Discard the garlic.

ADD the carrot, onion and celery to the saucepan and cook over moderate heat for 5–6 minutes, without browning. Increase the heat to high, add the wine and cook for 2–3 minutes. Add the stock, tomatoes and bouquet garni. Season with salt and pepper.

RETURN the veal shanks to the saucepan, standing them up in a single layer. Cover the pan, reduce the heat and simmer for 1 hour, or until the meat is tender and you can cut it with a fork.

IF YOU prefer a thicker sauce, remove the veal shanks and increase the heat. Boil the sauce until reduced and thickened, then return the veal to the saucepan. Discard the bouquet garni, and taste for salt and pepper.

VITELLO TONNATO

THERE ARE TWO VERSIONS OF THIS NORTH ITALIAN DISH, BOTH FEATURING A SAUCE OF MASHED
TUNA AND ANCHOVIES. IN THE OLDER, MILANESE, VERSION THE SAUCE IS THINNED WITH CREAM; THIS
RECIPE IS FOR THE PIEMONTESE DISH, WHICH USES MAYONNAISE RATHER THAN CREAM.

1 x 1.25 kg boneless rolled veal
    roast
500 ml dry white wine
500 ml chicken stock
2 garlic cloves
1 onion, quartered
1 carrot, roughly chopped
1 celery stalk, roughly chopped
2 bay leaves
3 cloves
10 peppercorns

SAUCE
95 g tin tuna in olive oil
15 g anchovy fillets
2 egg yolks
2 tablespoons lemon juice
125 ml olive oil

parsley sprigs
capers
thin lemon slices

SERVES 4

PUT the veal, wine, stock, garlic, onion, carrot,
celery, bay leaves, cloves and peppercorns in a
stockpot or very large saucepan. Add enough
water to come two-thirds of the way up the veal
and bring to the boil. Reduce the heat, cover the
saucepan and simmer for 1¼ hours, or until tender.
Leave to cool for 30 minutes, then remove the
veal from the pan and strain the stock. Pour the
stock into a saucepan and boil rapidly until
reduced to about 250 ml.

TO MAKE the sauce, purée the tuna and its oil
with the anchovy fillets in a blender or small food
processor. Add the egg yolks and 1 tablespoon of
the lemon juice and process until smooth. With
the motor running, slowly pour in the oil. Gradually
add the reduced stock until the sauce has the
consistency of a thin mayonnaise. (If you are
doing this by hand, chop the tuna and anchovy
finely, mix in the egg yolks and lemon juice and
then whisk in the oil and stock.) Blend in the
remaining lemon juice and season well.

TO SERVE, thinly slice the cold veal and arrange
in overlapping slices down the centre of a serving
platter. Spoon the sauce over the top and garnish
with the parsley, capers and lemon slices.

Capers are usually available
preserved in vinegar (these are
best rinsed before use) but you
will find that those preserved in
salt are of a superior quality. Rinse
well and pat dry before using.

The veal can be cooling in the
stock while you make the sauce.

VEAL INVOLTINI

INVOLTINI MEANS 'LITTLE BUNDLES' AND IF YOU TRAVEL AROUND ITALY YOU'LL FIND THIS RECIPE IN MANY GUISES. TRADITIONALLY INVOLTINI WERE MADE WITH MEAT OR FISH, STUFFED WITH BREADCRUMBS, PINENUTS AND CURRANTS. YOU COULD ALSO USE TURKEY OR CHICKEN BREAST.

Escalopes of veal are usually pounded with a meat mallet before use, giving a thin tender meat that can be wrapped around fillings and fried quickly. Tie the involtini with kitchen string to prevent them unravelling while you're frying.

8 asparagus spears
4 veal escalopes
4 thin slices mortadella (preferably with pistachio nuts)
4 thin slices Bel Paese
plain flour, seasoned with salt and pepper
3 tablespoons butter
1 tablespoon olive oil
3 tablespoons dry Marsala

SERVES 4

WASH the asparagus and remove the woody ends (hold each spear at both ends and bend it gently—it will snap at its natural breaking point). Blanch the asparagus in boiling salted water for 3 minutes. Drain, reserving 3 tablespoons of the liquid.

PLACE EACH veal escalope between two sheets of clingfilm and pound with a meat mallet to make a 12 x 18 cm rectangle. Season lightly with salt and pepper. Trim both the mortadella and cheese slices to just a little smaller than the veal.

COVER EACH piece of veal with a slice of mortadella, then a slice of cheese. Place an asparagus spear in the centre, running across the shortest width, with the tip slightly overhanging the veal at one end. Place another asparagus spear alongside, but with its tip overhanging the other end. Roll each veal slice up tightly and tie in place at each end with kitchen string. Roll in the seasoned flour to coat.

HEAT 2 tablespoons of the butter with the olive oil in a frying pan. Fry the rolls over low heat for about 10 minutes, turning frequently, until golden and tender. Transfer to a hot serving dish and keep warm.

ADD the Marsala, the reserved asparagus liquid and the remaining butter to the pan and bring quickly to the boil. Simmer for 3–4 minutes, scraping up the bits from the base of the pan. The juices will reduce and darken. Taste for seasoning, then spoon over the veal rolls and serve immediately.

UCCELLETTI SCAPPATI

THE NAME MEANS LITERALLY 'LITTLE BIRDS THAT GOT AWAY', EITHER BECAUSE IT IS FLAVOURED WITH SAGE AS BIRDS TRADITIONALLY WERE, OR BECAUSE IT LOOKS LIKE BIRDS ON A SKEWER. YOU CAN ALSO GRILL THE SKEWERS IF YOU PREFER, BASTING FREQUENTLY WITH MELTED BUTTER.

650 g sliced leg of veal
90 g pancetta, thinly sliced
50–60 sage leaves
90 g pancetta, cubed
75 g butter

SERVES 6

SOAK 12 bamboo skewers in cold water for 1 hour.

PLACE the veal between two sheets of clingfilm and pound with a meat mallet until an even thickness. Cut into 6 x 3 cm rectangles and trim the pancetta slices to the same size.

WORKING in batches, lie the veal pieces out flat on a board and season with pepper. Place a slice of pancetta on each rectangle of veal and then half a sage leaf on top. Roll each veal slice up, starting from one of the shortest ends.

THREAD a cube of pancetta onto a skewer, followed by a sage leaf. Thread the skewer through a veal roll to prevent it unrolling. Thread four more veal rolls onto the skewer, followed by a sage leaf and, finally, another cube of pancetta. Continue in this way with more skewers until all the ingredients are used.

HEAT the butter in a large frying pan. When it foams, add the skewers in batches and cook over high heat for about 12 minutes, or until cooked through, turning several times during cooking. Season lightly and serve with fried polenta.

Soak the skewers in water before you start to prevent them scorching (unless you're using metal skewers). Roll up the tiny bundles of veal, pancetta and sage and thread onto the skewers so they can't unroll. Wedge them in place at either end with a sage leaf and cube of pancetta.

Streets behind the Bay of Naples.

PICCATA AL LIMONE

4 large veal escalopes
plain flour, seasoned with salt and
    pepper
1 tablespoon olive oil
2 tablespoons butter
90 ml dry white wine
250 ml chicken stock
3 tablespoons lemon juice
2 tablespoons capers, rinsed and
    chopped if large
1 tablespoon finely chopped parsley
8 caperberries

SERVES 4

PLACE the veal between two sheets of clingfilm and pound with a meat mallet until an even thickness. Lightly dust each side with flour.

HEAT the olive oil and butter in a large frying pan. Fry the escalopes over moderately high heat for about 2 minutes on each side, or until golden. Season and transfer to a warm plate.

ADD the wine to the pan, increase the heat to high and boil until there are just 3–4 tablespoons of liquid left. Pour in the stock and boil for 4–5 minutes, or until it has reduced and slightly thickened. Add the lemon juice and capers and cook, stirring, for 1 minute. Taste for seasoning, then return the escalopes to the pan and heat through for 30 seconds. Sprinkle with parsley and serve at once, garnished with caperberries.

BISTECCA ALLA PIZZAIOLA

4 rib or rump steaks
4 tablespoons olive oil
560 g tomatoes
3 garlic cloves, crushed
3 basil leaves, torn into pieces
1 teaspoon finely chopped parsley

SERVES 4

BRUSH the steaks with 1 tablespoon of the olive oil and season well. Put on a plate and set aside.

SCORE a cross in the top of each tomato. Plunge into boiling water for 20 seconds, then drain and peel the skin away from the cross. Chop the tomatoes, discarding the cores.

HEAT 2 tablespoons of the olive oil in a saucepan over low heat and add the garlic. Soften without browning for 1–2 minutes, then add the tomato and season. Increase the heat, bring to the boil and cook for 5 minutes. Stir in the basil.

HEAT the remaining oil in a large frying pan with a tight-fitting lid. Brown the steaks over moderately high heat for 2 minutes on each side (cook in batches rather than overcrowding the pan). Place in a slightly overlapping row down the centre of the pan and spoon the sauce over the top, covering the steaks completely. Cover the pan and cook over low heat for about 5 minutes, or until the steaks are cooked to your taste. Sprinkle the parsley over the top and serve at once.

BISTECCA ALLA PIZZAIOLA

BOLLITO MISTO

THIS MEAL REQUIRES A TRIP TO A REALLY GOOD BUTCHER. IF YOU ARE LUCKY ENOUGH TO FIND A ZAMPONE (PORK SAUSAGE STUFFED INTO A PIG'S TROTTER), USE IT INSTEAD OF THE COTECHINO. YOU WILL ONLY NEED A LITTLE OF THE COOKING LIQUID FOR SERVING—KEEP THE REST FOR MAKING SOUP.

1 x 800 g cotechino sausage
1 x 1.25 kg small beef tongue
3 parsley sprigs
4 baby carrots
1 celery stalk, sliced
2 onions, roughly chopped
10 peppercorns
2 bay leaves
1 x 1.25 kg beef brisket
1 tablespoon tomato purée
1 x 900 g chicken
12 whole baby turnips
18 small onions, such as pickling
    or pearl onions

SERVES 8

BRING a saucepan of water to the boil. Prick the casing of the cotechino sausage and add to the pan. Reduce the heat, cover the saucepan and simmer for about 1 1/2 hours, or until tender. Leave in the cooking liquid until ready to use.

MEANWHILE, bring a stockpot or very large saucepan of water to the boil. Add the tongue, parsley, carrots, celery, chopped onion, peppercorns, bay leaves and 1 teaspoon salt. Bring back to the boil, skim the surface and add the beef brisket and tomato purée. Cover the pan, reduce the heat and simmer for 2 hours, skimming the surface from time to time.

ADD the chicken, turnips and onions to the stockpot and simmer for a further hour. Top up with boiling water if necessary to keep the meat always covered. Add the cotechino for the last 20 minutes of cooking.

TURN OFF the heat and remove the tongue. Peel, trim and slice it, then arrange the slices on a warm platter. Slice the cotechino and beef and quarter the chicken. Arrange all the meats on the platter and surround them with the carrots, turnips and onions. Moisten with a little of the cooking liquid then take to the table. Serve with salsa verde (page 285) and *mostarda di Cremona*.

'Boiled meats' is a tradition in prosperous northern Italy, where cows and pigs are plentiful, with Piemonte generally accepted as the home of the best bollito misto. There, grand restaurants serve seven different meats with three sauces from a special trolley. Elsewhere, and when cooked at home for large family gatherings, the dish is a little less flamboyant, containing only two or three different meats.

Wrapping the beef in prosciutto serves the dual purpose of sealing in the flavours of the garlic and rosemary and protecting the beef from the heat of the oven so it remains moist and juicy.

BEEF BRAISED IN RED WINE

IF YOU ARE FORTUNATE ENOUGH TO HAVE A WHOLE FILLET (RATHER THAN A PIECE OF ONE) THEN FOLD THE THIN END UNDER SO THE BEEF IS AN EVEN THICKNESS AND INCREASE THE QUANTITIES OF THE OTHER INGREDIENTS ACCORDINGLY. SERVE WITH CREAMY POLENTA.

750 g trimmed thick beef fillet
3 garlic cloves, thinly sliced
2 tablespoons chopped rosemary
8–10 thin slices prosciutto,
   pancetta or smoked bacon
2 tablespoons olive oil
20 g dried wild mushrooms, such
   as porcini
1 onion, halved and sliced
150 ml red wine such as Barolo
400 g tin chopped tomatoes

SERVES 4

MAKE SEVERAL small incisions around the beef. Push a slice of garlic into each incision, using up one of the garlic cloves. Scatter 1 tablespoon of rosemary over the beef and season with salt and pepper. Lay the prosciutto slices on a board in a line next to each other, creating a sheet of prosciutto to wrap the beef in. Put the beef fillet across them and fold the prosciutto over to enclose the fillet. Tie several times with kitchen string to keep the beef and prosciutto together. Leave in the fridge to rest for at least 15 minutes.

PREHEAT the oven to 190°C (375°F/Gas 5). Heat the olive oil in a casserole. Add the beef and sear on all sides until the prosciutto is golden brown, but not burnt. A little of the prosciutto might fall off, but it doesn't matter: just make sure the beef is well sealed. Remove from the casserole.

LEAVE the mushrooms to soak in 200 ml hot water for 10 minutes. Add the onion to the casserole, reduce the heat and gently cook until soft. Add the remaining garlic and rosemary and cook for a few minutes more.

REMOVE the mushrooms from the water and add to the onion, reserving the water. Cook the mushrooms for a couple of minutes, then add the mushroom water, discarding any sediment at the bottom of the bowl, and boil until nearly all the liquid is reduced. Add the wine and cook for a few minutes, then add the tomatoes and cook for a further 5–10 minutes to reduce to a thick sauce.

SEASON WITH salt and pepper and add the beef to the casserole, turning over in the sauce to coat all sides. Cover the casserole with a lid and place in the oven. Cook the beef for 15 minutes for rare or 20 minutes for medium-rare. Remove from the oven and leave to rest, covered, for at least 15 minutes.

BEEF COOKED IN RAGU

THIS DISH IS BOTH STARTER AND MAIN COURSE IN ONE POT. SERVE THE RAGU ON SPAGHETTI OR BUCATINI AS A FIRST COURSE, AND THE BEEF WITH VEGETABLES OR A SALAD FOR THE MAIN. RAGU IS THE TRADITIONAL TOMATO-BASED SAUCE OF BOLOGNA.

1 x 1.5 kg piece of beef, such as top rump or silverside
60 g pork fat, cut into small thin pieces
30 g butter
3 tablespoons olive oil
pinch of cayenne pepper
2 garlic cloves, finely chopped
2 onions, finely chopped
2 carrots, finely chopped
1 celery stalk, finely chopped
1/2 red pepper, finely chopped
3 leeks, sliced
185 ml red wine
1 tablespoon tomato purée
375 ml beef stock
200 ml tomato passata
8 basil leaves, torn into pieces
1/2 teaspoon finely chopped oregano leaves, or 1/4 teaspoon dried oregano
2 tablespoons finely chopped parsley
60 ml double cream

SERVES 6

MAKE DEEP incisions all over the beef with the point of a sharp knife, then push a piece of pork fat into each incision.

HEAT the butter and olive oil in a large casserole and brown the beef for 10–12 minutes, until it is browned all over. Season with salt and add the cayenne, garlic, onion, carrot, celery, pepper and leek. Cook over moderate heat for 10 minutes until the vegetables are lightly browned.

INCREASE the heat, add the wine and boil until it has evaporated. Stir in the tomato purée, then add the stock. Simmer for 30 minutes. Add the passata, basil and oregano and season with pepper. Cover the casserole and cook for about 1 hour, or until the beef is tender.

REMOVE the beef from the casserole and allow to rest for 10 minutes before carving. Taste the sauce for salt and pepper and stir in the parsley and cream.

The casserole needs to be large enough to hold the beef without it touching the side, so the sauce can cover the beef completely. Finish the sauce off with a little cream to make it velvety.

PORK BRAISED IN MILK

ASK YOUR BUTCHER TO CHINE AND SKIN THE PORK LOIN (CHINING MEANS REMOVING THE BACKBONE FROM THE RACK OF RIBS SO THAT YOU CAN CARVE BETWEEN THE RIBS). THE MILK AND LEMON SAUCE WILL APPEAR LUMPY AND CURDLED, BUT TASTES DELICIOUS—YOU CAN STRAIN IT IF YOU LIKE.

1 x 2.25 kg pork loin, chined and
   skinned
50 ml olive oil
4 garlic cloves, cut in half
   lengthways
15 g sage or rosemary leaves
1 litre milk
grated zest of 2 lemons
juice of 1 lemon

SERVES 6

PREHEAT the oven to 200°C (400°F/Gas 6). Prepare the pork by trimming the fat to leave just a thin layer. The bone and fat keeps the pork moist.

HEAT the olive oil in a large roasting tin. Add the pork and brown the meat on all sides. Remove the pork and pour away the fat from the roasting tin. Add the garlic and sage to the tin and place the pork on top of them. Season with salt and pepper and pour the milk over the pork. Return to the heat and bring just to the boil. Remove the tin from the heat again, add the lemon zest and drizzle with the lemon juice.

TRANSFER to the oven and roast for about 20 minutes. Reduce the temperature to 150°C (300°F/Gas 2) and cook for a further 1–1¼ hours, depending on the thickness of the meat. If necessary, add a little more milk every so often, to keep the meat roasting in liquid. Baste the meat with the juices every 30 minutes. Do not cover, so that the juices reduce and the fat on the pork becomes crisp.

TO TEST if the pork is cooked, poke a skewer into the middle of the meat, count to ten and pull it out. Touch it on the inside of your wrist and, if it feels hot, the meat is cooked through. Leave the meat to rest for 10 minutes before carving.

STRAIN the sauce if you like (you don't need to, but it may look curdled) and serve with the meat. Delicious with braised fennel, cavolo nero or roasted vegetables.

Putting the garlic and sage in the tin and laying the pork on top makes a rack for the meat to prevent it boiling in its own juices instead of roasting. Pour the milk over the pork and roast uncovered so the skin crisps.

FLORENTINE ROAST PORK

3 large fennel bulbs
1/2 tablespoon finely chopped
  rosemary
4 garlic cloves, crushed
1 x 1.5 kg pork loin, chined and
  skinned
3 white onions
90 ml olive oil
185 ml dry white wine
80 ml extra virgin olive oil
250 ml chicken stock
3–4 tablespoons double cream

SERVES 6

PREHEAT the oven to 200°C (400°F/Gas 6). Cut the green fronds from the tops of the fennel and chop to give 2 tablespoons. Mix with the rosemary, garlic and plenty of salt and black pepper. Make deep incisions with a sharp knife all over the pork and rub this mixture into the incisions and the splits in the pork bone. Cut two of the onions in half and place in a roasting tin. Put the pork on top of the onion and drizzle the olive oil over the top.

ROAST in the oven for 30 minutes. Baste the pork with the pan juices, then reduce the temperature to 180°C (350°F/Gas 4). Roast for a further 30 minutes. Baste and lightly salt the surface of the pork. Pour in half the white wine. Continue roasting for another 30–45 minutes, basting once or twice.

MEANWHILE, remove the tough outer leaves of the fennel and discard. Slice the bulbs vertically into 1 cm sections and place in a large saucepan. Thinly slice the remaining onion and add to the saucepan with the extra virgin olive oil and a little salt. Add enough water to cover, put the lid on and bring to the boil. Simmer for about 45 minutes, or until the fennel is creamy and soft and almost all the liquid has evaporated.

REMOVE the pork from the tin and leave to rest in a warm spot. Spoon off the excess oil from the tin and discard the onion. Place the tin over high heat on the stovetop and stir in the remaining wine to deglaze. Add the stock and boil the sauce until slightly thickened. Remove from the heat, season with salt and pepper and stir in the cream. Slice the pork and serve on the fennel, with the sauce.

Scoring the pork all over and pressing the fennel, garlic and rosemary into the cuts ensures that the flavour infuses the meat while it cooks. Cook the chopped fennel separately until it is creamy.

Use your hands to combine the meatball mixture—it's the easiest and most efficient method.

Lunching *al fresco* in Bologna.

ITALIAN MEATBALLS WITH TOMATO SAUCE

JUST ABOUT EVERY ITALIAN HOME WILL HAVE THEIR OWN FAMILY RECIPE FOR MEATBALLS, OR *POLPETTE*, AS THEY ARE KNOWN. THEY CAN BE SERVED WITH PASTA OR BREAD. THE DISH IS BEST MADE A DAY IN ADVANCE TO LET THE FLAVOURS BLEND TOGETHER.

180 ml olive oil
1 onion, finely chopped
100 g pine nuts, roughly chopped
3 garlic cloves, crushed
40 g parsley, roughly chopped
5 g basil or rosemary, roughly
    chopped
2 teaspoons fennel seeds, ground
50 g fresh breadcrumbs
250 g ricotta
25 g Parmesan, grated
grated zest of 1 large lemon
1 egg
500 g minced pork or beef

SAUCE
800 g tomatoes or 2 x 400 g tins
    tomatoes
100 ml red wine

SERVES 4

HEAT half the olive oil in a saucepan and cook the onion and pinenuts until the onion is soft and the pinenuts are light golden brown. Add the garlic and cook for a few minutes more, then set aside to cool.

PUT the herbs, fennel seeds, breadcrumbs, ricotta, Parmesan, lemon zest and egg in a bowl and add the mince. Add the cooled onion and pine nuts, season with salt and pepper and mix briefly until all the ingredients are combined. Test for correct seasoning by frying one small meatball and tasting for flavour. Leave the mixture to rest in the fridge for at least 30 minutes or overnight.

TO MAKE the meatballs, roll about 50 g of mixture into a ball about the size of a walnut and then flatten slightly to make it easier to cook on both sides. Repeat with the rest of the mixture.

HEAT the remaining olive oil in a large saucepan and fry the meatballs until golden brown on both sides. If necessary, cook them in two batches to prevent the pan overcrowding. Make sure there is enough oil to prevent the meatballs sticking to the base of the saucepan. Remove all the meatballs from the pan.

TO MAKE the sauce, if you are using fresh tomatoes, score a cross in the top of each one, plunge them into boiling water for 20 seconds, then drain and peel the skin away from the cross. Finely chop the flesh. Add the tomatoes and wine to the saucepan, season with salt and pepper and simmer for 5 minutes. Gently add the meatballs to the sauce and reduce the heat to a gentle simmer. Cover the saucepan and cook for a further 10 minutes. Leave for 10 minutes before serving.

ROAST LAMB

THIS RECIPE CAN ALSO BE USED FOR ROASTING A LEG OF VEAL OR A RIB OR LOIN OF LAMB OR VEAL. FOR LAMB, FOLLOW THE COOKING TIMES IN THE RECIPE. YOU WILL NEED TO ROAST THE VEAL FOR 25 MINUTES PER 450 GRAMS, PLUS AN EXTRA 10 MINUTES.

2 rosemary sprigs
3 garlic cloves
75 g pancetta
1 x 2 kg leg of lamb, shank bone
    cut off just above the joint and
    trimmed of excess fat
1 large onion, cut into 4 thick slices
125 ml olive oil
375 ml dry white wine

SERVES 4

PREHEAT the oven to 230°C (450°F/Gas 8).

STRIP the leaves off the rosemary sprigs and chop with the garlic and pancetta until fine and paste-like (a food processor works well for this). Season with a little salt and plenty of pepper.

WITH the point of a sharp knife, make incisions about 1 cm deep all over the lamb. Rub the rosemary filling over the surface of the lamb, pressing it into the incisions.

PUT the onion slices in the centre of a roasting tin. Place the lamb on top and gently pour the olive oil over it. Roast for 15 minutes. Reduce the temperature to 180°C (350°F/Gas 4) and pour in 250 ml of the wine. Roast for 1 hour for medium-rare, or longer if you prefer. Baste a couple of times and add a little water if the juices start to burn in the tin. Transfer the lamb to a carving platter and leave to rest for 10 minutes.

DISCARD the onion and spoon off the excess fat from the tin. Place over high heat on the stovetop, pour in the remaining wine and cook for 3–4 minutes, or until the sauce reduces and slightly thickens. Taste for seasoning. Slice the lamb and serve on a warm serving platter with the sauce spooned over the top.

Firmly but gently push the knife 1 cm into the meat at regular intervals. Baste a couple of times while the meat is roasting.

A butcher trims a leg of lamb in a Sicilian market.

SPICY LAMB CASSEROLE

THE PINCH OF CHILLI SIGNIFIES THIS AS A SOUTHERN DISH, PROBABLY FROM BASILICATA, WHERE SHEEP WERE THE MAIN SOURCE OF INCOME. SUCH DISHES OFTEN ORIGINATED WITH SHEPHERDS, WHO USED WILD HERBS AND VEGETABLES FOUND AROUND THEIR CAMP.

3 tablespoons olive oil
1.25 kg lamb leg or shoulder, cut
   into 4 cm cubes
1 small onion, finely chopped
1 celery stalk, finely chopped
3 garlic cloves, crushed
125 ml dry Marsala
3/4 teaspoon chilli flakes
1 tablespoon crushed juniper
   berries
2 tablespoons tomato purée
250 ml chicken stock
1 rosemary sprig
12 small onions, such as cipolline
   or pearl onions
2 potatoes, cut into cubes
2 tablespoons finely chopped
   parsley

SERVES 4

PREHEAT the oven to 180°C (350°F/Gas 4).

HEAT the olive oil in a large casserole. Add the lamb in batches, so that you don't overcrowd the pan, season with salt and pepper and brown lightly over high heat. Remove each batch from the casserole as it browns. Once all the lamb is browned and has been removed from the casserole, add the onion, celery and garlic, reduce the heat and cook for 4–5 minutes until softened.

RETURN the lamb to the casserole. Pour in the Marsala and cook over high heat until it is dark brown and reduced by half. Add the chilli flakes and juniper berries and cook, stirring, for just 10–15 seconds. Add the tomato purée, chicken stock, rosemary and about 250 ml water, or enough to just cover.

COVER the casserole with a lid and bake in the oven for 45 minutes. Add the onions and potato and cook for another 45 minutes. Stir the parsley through just before serving.

SAUSAGE AND LENTIL STEW

3 tablespoons olive oil
850 g Italian sausages
1 onion, chopped
3 garlic cloves, thinly sliced
1¹/₂ tablespoons chopped
   rosemary
800 g tin chopped tomatoes
16 juniper berries, lightly crushed
pinch of grated nutmeg
1 bay leaf
1 dried chilli, crushed
200 ml red wine
100 g green lentils

SERVES 4

HEAT the oil in a large saucepan and cook the sausages for 5–10 minutes, until browned. Remove the sausages from the pan and reduce the heat. Add the onion and garlic to the pan and cook gently until the onion is soft.

STIR IN the rosemary, then add the tomatoes and cook gently until reduced to a thick sauce. Add the juniper berries, nutmeg, bay leaf, chilli, wine and 400 ml water. Bring to the boil, then add the lentils and sausages. Give the stew a good stir, cover the pan and simmer gently for about 40 minutes, or until the lentils are soft. Stir a couple of times to prevent the lentils sticking to the base of the pan. Add a little more water if the lentils are still not cooked.

Umbria is the fertile heart of Italy and the tiny lentils that come from Castelluccio are regarded as the country's best. Traditionally, they are eaten on New Year's Eve to bring wealth in the coming year.

SAUSAGES WITH BROCCOLI

850 g Italian sausages
600 g broccoli, cut into florets
1 teaspoon olive oil
2 shallots, finely chopped
3 garlic cloves, crushed
¹/₄ red chilli, finely chopped
125 ml chicken stock
1 tablespoon lemon juice
6 pitted black olives

SERVES 4

PRICK the sausages several times, place in a single layer in a deep non-stick frying pan and add cold water to a depth of 1.5 cm. Bring to the boil, then reduce the heat and simmer for 20 minutes. Turn the sausages from time to time and add a little extra water should it evaporate too quickly—when the sausages are cooked, all the water will have evaporated, leaving just a little sausage fat in the pan.

MEANWHILE, bring a large saucepan of water to the boil. Add the broccoli with a teaspoon of salt. Simmer for 4–5 minutes, or until the florets are barely tender. Drain and set aside.

ADD the oil to the frying pan and evenly brown the sausages. Push to one side and add the shallots, garlic and chilli to the pan. Cook over low heat for 3–4 minutes, stirring from time to time. Add the stock and lemon juice, increase the heat and cook until reduced by half. Add the broccoli and olives, spoon the sauce over the broccoli and serve when it has heated through.

SAUSAGES WITH BROCCOLI

Saint Theodore taming the dragon in the Piazzetta San Marco, Venice.

LAMB KIDNEYS WITH FENNEL

20 lamb kidneys
90 ml vinegar
2 tablespoons olive oil
2 tablespoons butter
2 large onions, finely sliced
1 small fennel bulb, finely sliced
3 tablespoons finely chopped
  parsley
4 slices day-old 'country-style'
  bread, such as ciabatta, crusts
  removed
1 garlic clove, halved

SERVES 4

CUT the kidneys in half and place in a glass bowl. Add the vinegar and enough cold water to cover. Leave for at least 30 minutes.

MEANWHILE, heat the olive oil and butter in a large frying pan. Add the onion and fennel, season well and cook over very low heat without browning for 20–25 minutes. Transfer to a bowl.

CORE the kidneys and cut into thin slices. Add to the dry pan and cook over medium heat until they release their red liquid and turn brown. Drain through a colander, discarding the liquid. Rinse the kidneys under cold water and drain well.

WIPE the pan dry with paper towels, then add the cooked onion mixture and kidneys. Add the parsley and season well. Cook over moderately high heat, stirring often, for 3–4 minutes or until the kidneys brown.

TOAST the bread and rub with the cut side of the garlic. Serve with the kidneys.

VENETIAN LIVER

2 tablespoons olive oil
60 g butter
2 large onions, halved and thinly
  sliced
600 g calves liver, very thinly sliced
1 tablespoon finely chopped parsley
lemon wedges

SERVES 4

HEAT the olive oil and half the butter in a large frying pan and add the onion. Cover and cook over low heat for 30–40 minutes, stirring from time to time, until very soft and golden. Season well with salt and pepper and transfer to a bowl.

MELT the remaining butter in the frying pan, increase the heat and fry the liver quickly until brown on all sides. Return the onion to the pan and cook, stirring often, for 1–2 minutes more, or until the liver is cooked. Remove from the heat, stir in the parsley and check for seasoning. Serve with lemon wedges.

VENETIAN LIVER

VEGETABLES

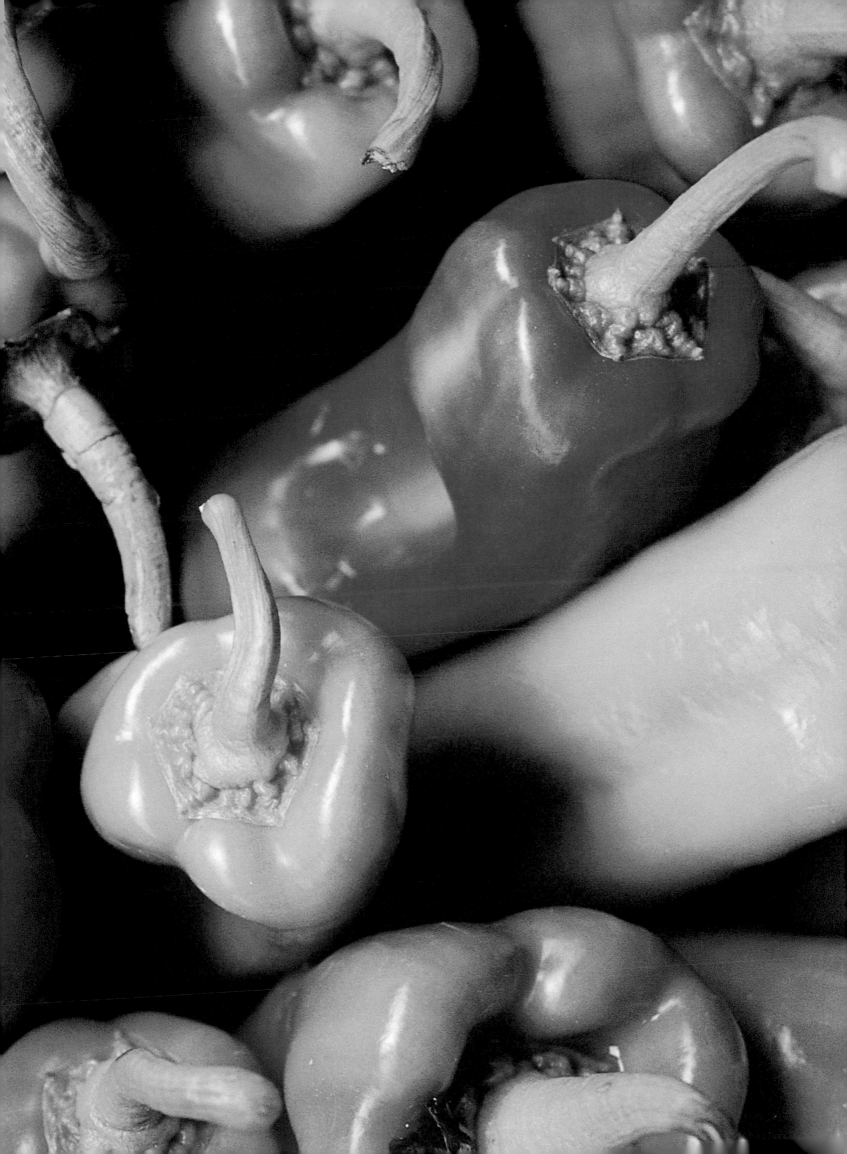

Frying the aubergine slices first adds flavour to the finished dish.

AUBERGINE PARMIGIANA

PARMIGIANA IS A DECEPTIVE NAME FOR THIS DISH, AS THE RECIPE DOES NOT, IN FACT, HAIL FROM THAT CITY. INSTEAD ITS CREATION IS CLAIMED BY ALMOST EVERY REGION OF ITALY, BUT THE USE OF MOZZARELLA AND TOMATOES INDICATES A DISH FROM THE SOUTH.

1.5 kg aubergines
plain flour
350 ml olive oil
500 ml tomato passata
2 tablespoons roughly torn basil
  leaves
250 g mozzarella, grated
90 g Parmesan, grated

SERVES 8

THINLY SLICE the aubergines lengthways. Layer the slices in a large colander, sprinkling salt between each layer. Leave for 1 hour to extract the bitter juices. Rinse and pat the slices dry on both sides with paper towels. Coat the aubergine slices lightly with flour.

PREHEAT the oven to 180°C (350°F/Gas 4) and grease a 32 x 20 cm shallow casserole or baking tray.

HEAT 125 ml of the olive oil in a large frying pan. Quickly fry the aubergine in batches over moderately high heat until crisp and golden on both sides. Add more olive oil as needed, and drain well on paper towels as you remove each batch from the pan.

MAKE a slightly overlapping layer of aubergine slices over the base of the dish. Season with pepper. Spoon 4 tablespoons of passata over the aubergine and scatter a few pieces of basil on top. Sprinkle with some mozzarella, followed by some Parmesan. Continue with this layering until you have used up all the ingredients.

BAKE FOR 30 minutes. Remove from the oven and allow to cool for 30 minutes before serving.

LA BANDIERA

LA BANDIERA IS THE NAME OF THE ITALIAN FLAG. THIS DISH, FROM PUGLIA IN ITALY'S SOUTH, CONTAINS TOMATOES, ROCKET AND PASTA—THE RED, GREEN AND WHITE INGREDIENTS MIMIC THE COLOURS OF THE FLAG.

2 potatoes, cut into 2 cm cubes
300 g ditali, pennette or
    maccheroncini rigati
4 tablespoons olive oil
3 garlic cloves, crushed
1/2 teaspoon minced anchovy fillets
2 x 400 g tins tomatoes, roughly
    chopped
1/4 teaspoon sugar
2 tablespoons chopped basil leaves
45 g rocket leaves, torn into small
    pieces if large
2 tablespoons grated pecorino, plus
    a little extra for serving

SERVES 4

PUT a large saucepan of water on to boil. Add the potato with 1 teaspoon salt. When the potato has been boiling for 3–4 minutes, stir the pasta into the water and cook until *al dente*.

MEANWHILE, heat the oil, garlic and anchovies in a large frying pan over low heat for about 30 seconds. Before the garlic colours, add the tomato, sugar and basil. Increase the heat, season with salt and pepper and simmer until the pasta in the other pan has finished cooking.

DRAIN the potato and pasta and add to the tomato sauce. Add the rocket and pecorino, toss to coat and serve at once, with a little extra grated pecorino over the top.

The colours of the Italian flag are reflected in many dishes, as tomatoes, peppers and green vegetables are often eaten with white mozzarella and pasta.

BEANS WITH RED PEPPER

200 g broad beans
300 g ditali, pennette or
    maccheroncini rigati
80 ml oil
2 garlic cloves, crushed
1 red pepper, julienned
pinch of cayenne pepper
200 g mozzarella, diced
3 tablespoons grated pecorino

SERVES 4

BRING a large saucepan of water to the boil. Add the broad beans and cook for 2 minutes. Using a slotted spoon, transfer the beans to a bowl and cover with a plate. Stir the pasta into the boiling water with 1 teaspoon salt and cook until *al dente*. Meanwhile, peel off the broad bean skins.

HEAT the oil in a large frying pan and add the garlic and red pepper. Cook over low heat, without browning, for 2–3 minutes then add the cayenne pepper.

DRAIN the pasta and add to the frying pan with the broad beans, mozzarella and pecorino. Toss to coat and heat until the mozzarella just begins to melt. Season and serve.

BEANS WITH RED PEPPER

The popularity of the bean has spread from its home region of Tuscany (whose inhabitants are affectionately known as the 'bean-eaters') to embrace the whole country. Many varieties of bean are bought dried and need to be soaked overnight before use.

FAGIOLI ALL'UCCELLETTO

350 g dried cannellini beans
bouquet garni
125 ml olive oil
2 garlic cloves
1 sage sprig, or 1/2 teaspoon dried sage
4 ripe tomatoes, peeled and chopped
1 tablespoon balsamic vinegar

SERVES 6

SOAK the beans in cold water overnight, then drain. Place in a large saucepan of cold water with the bouquet garni and bring to the boil. Add 2 tablespoons of the olive oil, reduce the heat and simmer for 1 hour. Add 1 teaspoon of salt and 500 ml boiling water and cook for a further 30 minutes, or until tender. Drain.

CUT the garlic cloves in half and put in a large saucepan with the sage and the remaining oil. Gently heat to infuse the flavours, but do not fry. Add the tomato and simmer for 10 minutes, then discard the garlic and the sprig of sage.

ADD the beans, season well and simmer for 15 minutes. Add a little boiling water at first to keep the pan moist, but then let the liquid evaporate towards the end of cooking. Stir the vinegar through just before serving. Serve hot.

BRAISED BORLOTTI BEANS

THESE BEANS ARE BEST EATEN WARM OR COLD RATHER THAN PIPING HOT STRAIGHT FROM THE STOVE. THEY KEEP WELL IN THE FRIDGE FOR UP TO SIX DAYS, BUT, IF YOU ARE MAKING THEM IN ADVANCE, DON'T ADD THE PARSLEY UNTIL YOU ARE READY TO SERVE.

BRAISED BORLOTTI BEANS

350 g dried borlotti beans
440 ml dry red wine
1 small onion, finely chopped
3 cloves
125 ml olive oil
1 rosemary sprig
3 garlic cloves, crushed
pinch of chilli flakes
3 tablespoons chopped parsley

SERVES 6

SOAK the beans in cold water overnight, then drain. Place in a large saucepan and add the wine, onion, cloves, half the olive oil and 875 ml water. Cover and bring to the boil. Reduce the heat, remove the lid and simmer for 1 hour.

HEAT the remaining oil in a small saucepan. Strip the leaves off the rosemary sprig and chop finely. Place in the oil with the garlic and chilli and cook for 1 minute. Add to the beans and simmer for 30 minutes–1 hour, until the beans are tender.

DRAIN the beans, reserving the cooking liquid. Return the cooking liquid to the pan and simmer until it thickens. Season. Return the beans to the pan and simmer for a further 5 minutes. Stir in the parsley and cool for 15 minutes before serving.

CHARGRILLED RADICCHIO

2 heads radicchio
60 ml olive oil
1 teaspoon balsamic vinegar

SERVES 4

TRIM the radicchio, discarding the outer leaves. Slice into quarters lengthways and rinse well. Drain, then pat dry with paper towels.

PREHEAT a griddle to hot. Lightly sprinkle the radicchio with some of the olive oil and season. Cook for 2–3 minutes, until the under leaves soften and darken, then turn to cook the other side. Transfer to a dish and sprinkle with the remaining oil and vinegar. Serve hot with grilled meats, or cold as part of an antipasto platter.

There are several types of radicchio available in Italy, all from the North. This round variety, *rossa di Verona*, is from Chioggia. The longer-leaved type is from Treviso.

CARDOONS WITH PARMESAN

CARDOONS, LIKE ARTICHOKES, ARE A TYPE OF THISTLE, GROWN FOR THEIR STALKS. THEY BROWN WHEN CUT, SO USE A STAINLESS STEEL KNIFE AND KEEP THEM IN ACIDULATED WATER. THE SICILIANS ALSO CALL THE YOUNG STALKS OF ARTICHOKES CARDOONS AND COOK THEM IN THE SAME WAY.

juice of 1 lemon
750 g cardoons
1 tablespoon plain flour
60 g butter
1 small onion, thinly sliced
4 tablespoons grated Parmesan

SERVES 4

PUT HALF the lemon juice in a large bowl of cold water. Discard the green leaves, outer stalks and tough parts of the cardoons, leaving the tender white stalks. Cut into 8 cm lengths and toss into the bowl of water.

BRING a large saucepan of water to the boil. Add the remaining lemon juice, the flour and a large pinch of salt. Add the cardoons. Simmer for about 50 minutes, or until tender. Drain and plunge into a bowl of cold water. Remove the strings with a knife, as you would with celery.

PREHEAT the oven to 180°C (350°F/Gas 4) and grease a shallow 25 x 15 cm casserole or baking tray. Melt the butter in a small frying pan and add the onion. Cook over low heat for 10 minutes until soft and golden.

LAYER HALF the cardoons over the base of the casserole and season with pepper. Spoon half the onion over the top and sprinkle with half the Parmesan. Repeat these layers and bake in the oven for 30 minutes.

CARDOONS WITH PARMESAN

POTATO CAKE

THE SOUTH OF ITALY LOVES ITS PASTA, WHILE THE NORTH FAVOURS RICE AND POLENTA. ALTHOUGH THE POTATO HAS NEVER BECOME QUITE THE STAPLE IN ITALY THAT IT IS IN OTHER COUNTRIES, THERE ARE STILL SOME TRADITIONAL RECIPES.

1 small onion, thinly sliced into rings
75 g butter
2 garlic cloves, crushed
1 kg potatoes, thinly sliced
100 g mozzarella, grated
50 g Parmesan, grated
2 tablespoons milk

SERVES 4

PLACE the onion in a bowl, cover with cold water and leave for 1 hour. Drain well. Preheat the oven to 210°C (415°F/Gas 6–7). Line a 20 cm springform cake tin with foil. Grease the foil.

MELT the butter in a small saucepan, add the garlic and set aside. Place a layer of potato over the base of the tin, followed by layers of onion, butter, mozzarella and Parmesan. Repeat the layers until you have used up all the ingredients, finishing with potato and keeping a bit of butter to drizzle on at the end. Season the layers as you go. Spoon the milk over the top.

BAKE for 1 hour, or until the top is golden brown and the potatoes are tender. If the top is overbrowning before the potatoes are done, cover with foil. Cool for 10 minutes before serving. Unclip the base of the tin, peel off the foil and transfer to a warm plate for serving.

ROASTED ROSEMARY POTATOES

80 ml extra virgin olive oil
750 g floury potatoes, cut into
  4 cm cubes
long rosemary sprig
sea salt

SERVES 4

PREHEAT the oven to 170°C (325°F/Gas 3). Pour the oil into a shallow casserole or baking tray. Toss the potato into the casserole, turning to coat thoroughly in oil, then spread out so that the pieces aren't touching. Scatter the rosemary leaves over the potatoes.

ROAST for 30 minutes, then turn and sprinkle generously with sea salt. Return to the oven and roast for a further 30–40 minutes, or until crisp and golden. Serve hot or cold.

ROASTED ROSEMARY
POTATOES

POTATO AND LEEK GRATIN

3 tablespoons butter
400 g leeks, trimmed, halved and
    sliced
3 garlic cloves, thinly sliced
1 tablespoon chopped thyme
1 kg potatoes, thinly sliced
350 g mascarpone
250 ml vegetable stock

SERVES 4

PREHEAT the oven to 180°C (375°F/Gas 4). Heat the butter in a saucepan and cook the leeks for 10 minutes until soft. Season, add the garlic and thyme and cook for a couple of minutes. Grease a 20 cm round gratin dish with butter.

ARRANGE a layer of potato in the base of the dish and season with salt and pepper. Scatter with 3 tablespoons of leek and a few dollops of mascarpone. Continue the layers, finishing with a layer of potato and some mascarpone. Pour the stock over the top and cover with foil.

BAKE for 45 minutes, then remove the foil and bake for a further 15 minutes to brown the top.

POTATO AND PUMPKIN GRATIN

450 g potatoes, thinly sliced
leaves from 3 large thyme or
    rosemary sprigs, finely chopped
700 g pumpkin, thinly sliced
1 large garlic clove, crushed
500 ml double cream

SERVES 4

PREHEAT the oven to 180°C (375°F/Gas 4). Lightly grease a 25 x 23 cm gratin dish with a little butter. Arrange a layer of potato in the dish, season with salt, pepper and herbs, then top with a layer of pumpkin. Continue the layers, finishing with pumpkin. Mix the garlic with the cream and pour over the top. Cover the dish with buttered foil and bake in the oven for about 45 minutes.

TEST TO see if the gratin is cooked by inserting a knife into the centre. If the slices seem soft, it is cooked. Remove the foil and increase the oven temperature to 190°C (375°F/Gas 5). Cook for a further 15 minutes, until there is a good brown crust on top. Leave to rest for at least 10 minutes before serving. Delicious with grilled meats or on its own with just a green salad.

POTATO AND PUMPKIN GRATIN

VEGETABLE TORTE

150 g asparagus
4 tablespoons olive oil
1 onion, chopped
1 courgette, halved lengthways and
    finely sliced
2 large garlic cloves, crushed
100 g spinach, stalks removed if
    necessary
1 tablespoon chopped basil
75 g Parmesan, grated
250 g ricotta
250 g mascarpone
4 eggs

SERVES 4

WASH the asparagus and remove the woody ends (hold each spear at both ends and bend it gently—it will snap at its natural breaking point). Remove the spear tips of the asparagus and slice the remaining stems. Bring a small saucepan of salted water to the boil and cook the asparagus stems for about 2 minutes. Add the tips and cook for 1 minute. Drain the asparagus and set aside.

PREHEAT the oven to 180°C (375°F/Gas 4). Heat the olive oil in a saucepan and cook the onion until soft. Increase the heat and add the courgette. Cook until the courgette is soft and golden brown, stirring occasionally. Add the garlic and cook for 1 minute more. Finally, add the spinach and mix briefly until just wilted.

REMOVE the pan from the heat, add the asparagus and the basil, season with salt and pepper and set aside to cool.

GREASE a 20 cm springform tin with butter and dust with about 1 tablespoon of the Parmesan. Mix together the ricotta, mascarpone, eggs and 50 g Parmesan and add it to the cooled vegetables. Mix well and taste for seasoning.

SPOON the mixture into the tin and scatter with the remaining Parmesan. Place in the oven, on a tray to catch any drips, and cook for about 30 minutes. The top should be light golden brown and the mixture still wobble slightly in the centre. Leave to cool for 30 minutes, then chill in the fridge for about 3 hours, until the torte has set. Serve with a simple rocket or mixed leaf salad.

PIZZAS & BREADS

Naples in the shadow of Vesuvius.

PIZZA SPINACI

2 tablespoons olive oil
2 garlic cloves, crushed
2 tablespoons pine nuts
1 kg spinach, roughly chopped
1 x 30 cm pizza base (page 281)
cornmeal
1 quantity tomato sauce (page 285)
220 g mozzarella, chopped
15 very small black olives, such as
   Ligurian
3 tablespoons grated Parmesan

MAKES ONE 30 CM PIZZA

PREHEAT the oven to 240°C (475°F/Gas 9). Heat the oil in a frying pan and fry the garlic and pine nuts over low heat until golden. Add the spinach, increase the heat and stir until wilted. Season.

PLACE the pizza base on a baking tray dusted with cornmeal and spoon the tomato sauce onto the base, spreading it up to the rim. Sprinkle with half the mozzarella. Spread the spinach and olives over the top, followed by the rest of the mozzarella and the Parmesan.

BAKE for 12–15 minutes, or until golden and puffed. Brush the rim with a little extra olive oil before serving.

PIZZA MARGHERITA

THIS CLASSIC PIZZA WAS SUPPOSEDLY INVENTED IN 1889 BY RAFFAELE ESPOSITO IN HONOUR OF QUEEN MARGHERITA. THE QUEEN HAD HEARD SO MUCH OF THE FABLED PIZZAS OF NAPLES THAT SHE REQUESTED ONE TO EAT WHEN SHE VISITED THE CITY.

1 x 30 cm pizza base (page 281)
cornmeal
1 quantity tomato sauce (page 285)
150 g mozzarella, chopped
9 small basil leaves
1 tablespoon olive oil

MAKES ONE 30 CM PIZZA

PREHEAT the oven to 240°C (475°F/Gas 9). Place the pizza base on a baking tray dusted with cornmeal and spoon the tomato sauce onto the base, spreading it up to the rim. Scatter with the mozzarella and basil and drizzle with the oil.

BAKE for 12–15 minutes, or until golden and puffed. Remove from the oven and brush the rim with a little extra olive oil before serving.

PIZZA MARGHERITA

PIZZA QUATTRO STAGIONI

1 x 30 cm pizza base (page 281)
cornmeal
1 quantity tomato sauce (page 285)
1 tablespoon grated Parmesan
60 g mozzarella, chopped
30 g thinly sliced prosciutto, cut into
    small pieces
1 plum tomato, thinly sliced
3 basil leaves, shredded
4 small artichoke hearts, marinated
    in oil, drained and quartered
4 button mushrooms, sliced
pinch of dried oregano
1 tablespoon olive oil

MAKES ONE 30 CM PIZZA

PREHEAT the oven to 240°C (475°F/Gas 9). Place the pizza base on a baking tray dusted with cornmeal and spoon the tomato sauce onto the base, spreading it up to the rim. Sprinkle the Parmesan on top.

VISUALLY divide the pizza into quarters. Scatter the mozzarella over two opposite quarters. Spread the prosciutto over one of these, and arrange the tomato over the other. Lightly salt the tomato and sprinkle on the basil.

ARRANGE the artichoke over the third quarter, and the mushrooms over the final quarter. Sprinkle the oregano over both these sections.

DRIZZLE the oil over the pizza. Bake for 12–15 minutes, or until golden and puffed.

Italy is the world's largest producer of artichokes, with 98 per cent of the crop being grown for export. This beautiful vegetable, which varies in colour from green to vibrant purple, is actually a thistle.

PIZZA MELANZANA

220 g long thin aubergines, thinly
    sliced
60 ml olive oil
1 x 30 cm pizza base (page 281)
cornmeal
1 quantity tomato sauce (page
    285), made with a pinch of chilli
    flakes
170 g mozzarella, chopped
15 black olives
1 tablespoon capers
4 tablespoons grated pecorino
1 tablespoon olive oil

MAKES ONE 30 CM PIZZA

LAYER the aubergine in a colander, sprinkling salt on each layer. Leave to drain for 1 hour. Wipe off the salt with paper towels. Preheat the oven to 240°C (475°F/Gas 9).

HEAT the olive oil in a large frying pan and quickly brown the aubergine on both sides, cooking in batches. Drain on paper towels.

PLACE the pizza base on a baking tray dusted with cornmeal and spoon the tomato sauce onto the base, spreading it up to the rim. Arrange the aubergine in a circular pattern over the top, then scatter with mozzarella. Cover with the olives, capers and pecorino, then drizzle with the oil. Bake for 12–15 minutes, or until golden and puffed.

PIZZA MELANZANA

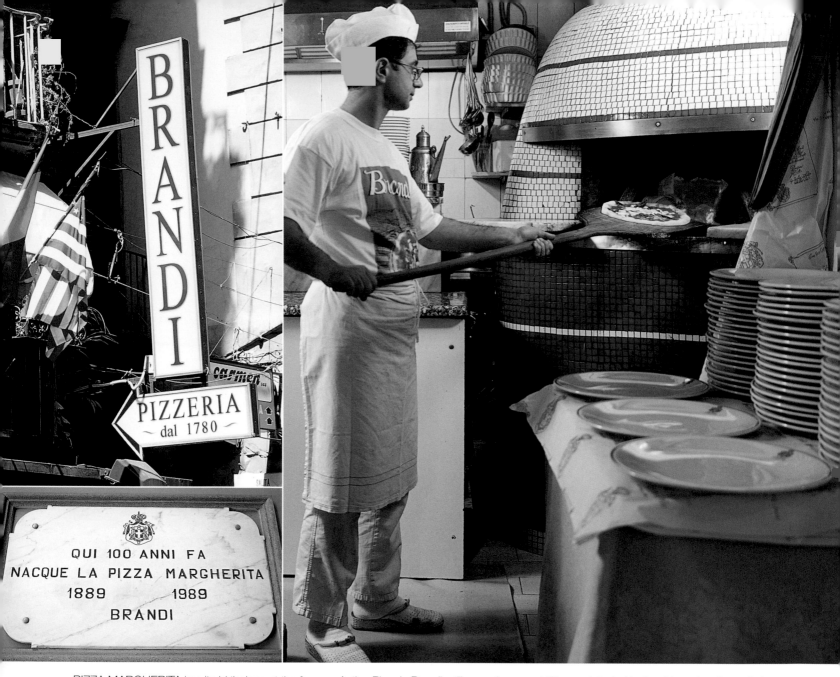

PIZZA MARGHERITA has its birthplace at the famous Antica Pizzeria Brandi, still operating over 100 years later in Naples. Here pizza is made by hand, following the traditional methods. The kitchen is open so customers can see the work of the *pizzaiolo* and the brick-lined wood-fired pizza oven is kept at such a high temperature and is so thick that it retains its heat overnight. Each pizza takes only 1 or 2 minutes to brown and puff up.

PIZZA

PIZZA BEGAN LIFE AS A FAST FOOD, EATEN HOT ON THE BACKSTREETS OF NAPLES. TODAY IT IS FOUND ALL OVER THE WORLD, BUT IT IS STILL IN NAPLES THAT SKILLED *PIZZAIOLI* (PIZZA-MAKERS) USE WONDERFUL LOCAL TOMATOES, MOZZARELLA AND BASIL TO PRODUCE THE FINEST OF PIZZAS.

A pizza, in the sense of a flat bread covered with toppings, has probably been around since the Greeks and Romans, and many regions developed their own versions. However, it is the pizza of Naples that has come to be regarded as the true pizza. The first Neapolitan pizzas were white, made with garlic, lard, salt and anchovies. It was the tomato that was to transform pizza and the Neapolitans who were the first Europeans to embrace this new fruit, successfully growing them from seeds brought from the New World. The first tomato pizza was probably the classic *marinara*.

PIZZA MARGHERITA

By the mid-nineteenth century, pizzerias had opened in Naples and wandering vendors sold slices to people on the streets. A way of life was born for the Neapolitans and their pizza began to achieve wider notoriety, with visitors venturing into poor neighbourhoods to sample this new food. When Queen Margherita visited in 1889, she too wanted to try the famous pizza. A *pizzaiolo,* Raffaele Esposito, was summoned and created a pizza of mozzarella, tomatoes and basil based on the colours of the Italian flag—later to be named after her.

PIZZA IS THE CLASSIC fast food and in Naples traditional round pizzas are baked to order, then folded into quarters and wrapped in paper to take away. Elsewhere, it is more usual to find *pizza a tagglio,* pizza that has been baked in a large tray and then sold by the slice. Probably originating in Rome, *pizza a tagglio* can be ordered by weight in many places and is then reheated as a fast snack or lunch.

ASSOCIAZIONE VERA PIZZA NAPOLETANA

The True Neapolitan Pizza Association has been set up to safeguard the pizza. Their guidelines include that the dough must be made only from flour, yeast, salt and water and not be worked by machine. Pizzas are to be cooked directly on the floor of a brick or stone-lined wood-fired oven and the temperature must exceed 400°C (750°F). The *cornicione* (border) must be high and soft and the whole crust not too crisp. A pizza should take only 2 minutes to cook and be brown and crispy with all the ingredients melted together.

Emigrating Neapolitans took pizza with them to America and, by the 1950s, pizza could probably be found more easily in America than in the north of Italy. When the rest of Italy did finally take to pizza, they adapted it to their own tastes: the Roman pizza has more topping, is thinner and crisper and does not have a *cornicione.*

CALZONE

CALZONE DIFFERS FROM A PIZZA IN THAT THE BASE IS FOLDED OVER THE TOPPING. THIS NEAPOLITAN SPECIALITY MEANS 'TROUSER LEG', PRESUMABLY BECAUSE THERE IS A RESEMBLANCE. EACH OF THE FOLLOWING FILLINGS MAKES ONE 25 CM CALZONE—ENOUGH FOR ONE TO TWO PEOPLE.

cornmeal
1/2 quantity pizza dough (page 281)
  for each calzone
1 1/2 tablespoons olive oil

MOZZARELLA AND PROSCIUTTO
170 g mozzarella, cut into 2 cm
  cubes
2 thin slices prosciutto, cut in half
1 artichoke heart, marinated in oil,
  drained and cut into 3 slices from
  top to bottom

POTATO, ONION AND SALAMI
2 tablespoons vegetable oil
1 small onion, very thinly sliced
75 g small red potatoes, unpeeled,
  very thinly sliced
75 g mozzarella, chopped
60 g sliced salami
2 tablespoons grated Parmesan

EACH RECIPE MAKES
ONE 25 CM CALZONE

PREHEAT the oven to 230°C (450°F/Gas 8). Lightly oil a baking tray and dust with cornmeal.

ON a lightly floured surface roll out the dough into an 18 cm circle. Now, using the heels of your hands and working from the centre outwards, press the circle out to a diameter of about 30 cm. Transfer to the baking tray. Brush the entire surface lightly with the oil.

TO MAKE the mozzarella and prosciutto calzone, spread the mozzarella cheese over one half of the pizza base, leaving a narrow border around the edge. Roll the half slices of prosciutto into little tubes and place on top of the cheese. Top with the artichoke slices, then season well.

TO MAKE the potato, onion and salami calzone, heat the oil in a frying pan and add the onion slices. Cook for 1 minute, then scatter the potato on top. Cook, stirring, for 3–4 minutes, until beginning to brown. Season with salt and pepper. Spread over one half of the pizza base, leaving a narrow border around the edge. Scatter the mozzarella on top, followed by the salami slices and Parmesan.

WHICHEVER calzone you are making, now fold the plain side of the base over the filling to make a half-moon shape. Match the cut edges and press them firmly together to seal. Fold them over and press into a scrolled pattern to thoroughly seal in the filling. Brush the surface with a little extra olive oil, then transfer to the oven. Bake for about 20 minutes, until the crust is golden.

POTATO, ONION AND
SALAMI CALZONE

MOZZARELLA AND PROSCIUTTO CALZONE

FOCACCIA WITH GREEN OLIVES AND ROSEMARY

ONE QUANTITY OF THE FOCACCIA DOUGH RECIPE (PAGE 282) MAKES TWO FOCACCIA. EACH OF THE FOLLOWING RECIPES IS FOR ONE FOCACCIA, SO YOU CAN MAKE A COUPLE OF DIFFERENT TYPES WITH EACH QUANTITY OF DOUGH.

FOCACCIA WITH GREEN OLIVES AND ROSEMARY

1/2 quantity focaccia dough (page 282), rolled out and on a tray
185 g green olives
olive oil
2 teaspoons coarse sea salt
leaves of 2 rosemary sprigs

MAKES 1 FOCACCIA

PREHEAT the oven to 220°C (425°F/Gas 7). When the dough has risen a second time, scatter the olives over the surface and press them firmly down into the dough.

BRUSH WITH olive oil and sprinkle with the salt and rosemary. Bake for about 20 minutes, or until golden.

FOCACCIA WITH PANCETTA AND PARMESAN

1/2 quantity focaccia dough (page 282), rolled out and on a tray
90 g pancetta, diced
10 basil leaves, torn in half
olive oil
2 tablespoons grated Parmesan

MAKES 1 FOCACCIA

PREHEAT the oven to 220°C (425°F/Gas 7). When the dough has risen a second time, scatter the pancetta over the surface and press the pieces firmly into the dough. Press a piece of basil into each indentation. Brush the surface of the dough with olive oil, sprinkle with Parmesan and bake for about 20 minutes, or until golden.

FOCACCIA WITH GORGONZOLA AND PINE NUTS

150 g Gorgonzola, or other creamy blue cheese
1–3 tablespoons mascarpone
1/2 quantity focaccia dough (page 282), rolled out and on a tray
10 sage leaves, roughly chopped
2 tablespoons pine nuts

MAKES 1 FOCACCIA

PREHEAT the oven to 220°C (425°F/Gas 7). Roughly mash the Gorgonzola with a fork, then mix in enough mascarpone to make the cheese spreadable, but not thin. When the dough has risen a second time, spread the Gorgonzola over the surface. Scatter over the sage and pine nuts and bake for about 20 minutes, or until golden.

FOCACCIA WITH GORGONZOLA AND PINE NUTS

FOCACCIA WITH PANCETTA AND PARMESAN

COUNTRY-STYLE BREAD

THIS IS ONE OF THE BASIC LOAVES OF ITALY (ALTHOUGH NOT TUSCANY, WHERE THE REGIONAL *PANE TOSCANO* IS MADE WITHOUT SALT). IF YOU'RE SERVING IT FRESH WITH BUTTER, IT'S BEST EATEN ON BAKING DAY, BUT THE DAY-OLD BREAD IS EXCELLENT FOR MAKING BRUSCHETTA AND CROSTINI.

STARTER
185 ml milk, warmed
2 teaspoons honey
1 teaspoon dried yeast or
  7 g fresh yeast
125 g plain flour

DOUGH
1 teaspoon dried yeast or
  7 g fresh yeast
2 1/2 teaspoons salt
500 g plain flour

MAKES 2 LOAVES

TO MAKE the starter, mix the milk and honey in a large bowl with 3 tablespoons warm water. Sprinkle the yeast over the top and stir to dissolve. Leave in a draught-free spot to activate. If the yeast does not bubble and foam in 5 minutes, throw it away and start again. Add the flour and whisk to form a thick paste. Cover loosely with clingfilm and leave at room temperature overnight.

TO MAKE the dough, sprinkle the yeast over the starter. Using your fingertips, break up the starter by squeezing it between your fingers. Gradually add 250 ml water, combining it with the starter. Mix in the salt and flour with your fingers until the mixture comes together to form a soft dough.

TURN the dough out onto a lightly floured work surface and knead for 10 minutes or until smooth and elastic. Place the dough in a lightly oiled bowl and cover with a damp tea towel. Leave to rise in a draught-free place for 1–1 1/2 hours or until doubled in size. Knock back, turn out onto a lightly floured surface and knead for 1–2 minutes until smooth.

DIVIDE the dough into two and shape into round loaves, then flatten them slightly. Lightly grease a large baking tray with oil and dust with flour. Put the loaves on the tray and score a criss-cross pattern about 5 mm deep on top of each loaf. Dust lightly with more flour.

COVER with a damp tea towel and leave to rise in a draught-free place for about 40 minutes, or until doubled in size. Preheat the oven to 200°C (400°F/Gas 6). Bake for 30–35 minutes or until the bread sounds hollow when tapped underneath. Transfer to a wire rack to cool.

PIZZETTE

1/2 quantity pizza dough (page 281)
cornmeal
1 tablespoon olive oil
250 g mozzarella, grated

GARLIC AND ROSEMARY PIZZETTE
4 garlic cloves, crushed
2 teaspoons chopped rosemary
1 1/2 tablespoons olive oil
55 g Parmesan, grated
3 garlic cloves, thinly sliced

TOMATO AND OLIVE PIZZETTE
200 g pitted black olives, diced
400 g plum tomatoes, diced
3 garlic cloves, crushed
2 tablespoons finely shredded basil
3 tablespoons olive oil
5 small basil sprigs

MAKES 10 PIZZETTE

PREHEAT the oven to 240°C (475°C/Gas 9). Form the pizza dough into ten bases. Place the pizza bases on two baking trays dusted with cornmeal. Brush with the oil, then sprinkle the bases with mozzarella. Make five garlic and rosemary pizzette and five tomato and olive pizzette.

TO MAKE the garlic and rosemary pizzette, scatter five bases with the crushed garlic and rosemary and drizzle the oil over the top. Sprinkle with Parmesan and garnish with some slices of garlic.

TO MAKE the tomato and olive pizzette, mix together the olives, tomato, garlic and shredded basil and spoon over the remaining bases. Drizzle over the oil and garnish with the basil sprigs.

BAKE the pizzette for 10 minutes, or until the bases are crisp and golden.

An old olive oil press at the Ravida estate in Menfi in Sicily. This stone was turned by a donkey who walked around it in a circle. Olives were ground between the two stones before being pressed to extract the oil.

GRISSINI

1 tablespoon malt syrup
2 teaspoons dried yeast or 15 g
   fresh yeast
500 g plain flour
1 1/2 teaspoons salt
2 tablespoons olive oil
fine semolina

MAKES 20

PUT 310 ml warm water in a bowl and stir in the malt and yeast. Leave until the yeast foams. Sift the flour and salt into a bowl, add the yeast and the oil and mix until the dough clumps together.

FORM into a ball and knead on a lightly floured surface for 5–6 minutes, or until smooth and elastic. Put the dough on a lightly oiled tray and squash out to fill the shape of the tray. Brush with oil. Slide into a plastic bag and leave for 1 hour, or until doubled in size.

PREHEAT the oven to 230°C (450°F/Gas 8) and lightly oil two baking trays. Sprinkle the dough with semolina. Cut into four portions along its length, then slice each one into five strips. Pick up each strip by both ends and stretch out to 20 cm long. Place on the trays, 5 cm apart.

BAKE for 20 minutes, or until crisp and golden. Cool slightly on the trays and then on wire racks.

GRISSINI

POLENTA, RICE
& PASTA

POLENTA WITH WILD MUSHROOMS

POLENTA, MADE FROM COARSE-GROUND CORN, WAS KNOWN AS THE FOOD OF THE POOR IN ROMAN TIMES. TODAY, ESPECIALLY AMONG ITALIANS LIVING ABROAD, IT HAS A WIDE AND LOVING AUDIENCE. SOMETIMES POLENTA IS SO FINE IT IS ALMOST WHITE; MORE OFTEN IT IS GOLDEN YELLOW.

POLENTA
1 tablespoon salt
300 g coarse-grain polenta
50 g butter
75 g Parmesan, grated

50 ml olive oil
400 g selection of wild mushrooms,
   particularly fresh porcini, sliced
   if large, or chestnut mushrooms
2 garlic cloves, crushed
1 tablespoon chopped thyme
150 g mascarpone

SERVES 6

The fresh porcini is considered the king of mushrooms. Several different varieties are available and appear during the summer and autumn. Porcini are also dried and preserved in oil for the months they are not available.

BRING 1.5 litres water to the boil in a heavy-based saucepan and add the salt. Add the polenta to the water in a gentle stream, whisking or stirring vigorously as you pour it in. Reduce the heat immediately so that the water is simmering. Stir continuously for the first 30 seconds to avoid any lumps appearing—the more you stir, the better the texture will be. Once you have stirred well at the beginning you can leave the polenta to mildly bubble away, stirring it every few minutes to prevent it sticking. Cook for 40 minutes.

MEANWHILE, prepare the mushrooms. Heat the olive oil in a large saucepan or frying pan. When the oil is hot, add just enough mushrooms to cover the base of the pan and cook at quite a high heat, stirring frequently. Season with salt and pepper. Sometimes the mushrooms can become watery when cooked: just keep cooking until all the liquid has evaporated. Add a little of the garlic at the last minute to prevent it burning and then add a little thyme.

REMOVE THIS batch of mushrooms from the pan and repeat the process until they are all cooked. Return all the mushrooms to the pan (if the polenta isn't yet cooked, leave all the mushrooms in the pan and then reheat gently). Add the mascarpone and let it melt into the mushrooms.

ADD the butter and 50 g of the Parmesan to the cooked polenta and season with pepper. Spoon the polenta onto plates and then spoon the mushrooms on top. Sprinkle with the remaining Parmesan and serve immediately.

Santa Maria della Salute, Venice.

BAKED POLENTA WITH FOUR CHEESES

IF YOU HAVE TIME, USE 'PROPER' POLENTA INSTEAD OF THE QUICK-COOK VARIETY. IT MIGHT SEEM LABOUR INTENSIVE, AS YOU HAVE TO STIR CONSTANTLY, BUT THE FLAVOUR IS BETTER. IN ITALY THEY SOLVE THE PROBLEM BY HAVING SPECIAL 'SELF-STIRRING' POLENTA PANS WITH A REVOLVING SPOON.

POLENTA
1 tablespoon salt
300 g coarse-grain polenta
75 g butter

TOMATO SAUCE
3 tablespoons olive oil
2 garlic cloves, thinly sliced
15 g rosemary or thyme, roughly
   chopped
800 g tin tomatoes

200 g Gorgonzola, cubed
250 g Taleggio, cubed
250 g mascarpone
100 g Parmesan, grated

SERVES 6

BRING 1.5 litres water to the boil in a heavy-based saucepan and add the salt. Add the polenta to the water in a gentle stream, whisking or stirring vigorously as you pour it in. Reduce the heat immediately so that the water is simmering. Stir continuously for the first 30 seconds to avoid any lumps appearing—the more you stir, the better the texture will be. Once you have stirred well at the beginning you can leave the polenta to mildly bubble away, stirring it every few minutes to prevent it sticking. Cook for 40 minutes. Add the butter and mix well.

POUR the polenta into a shallow casserole or baking tray about 5 cm deep (you want the polenta to come no more than halfway up the side of the dish). Leave to cool completely.

TO MAKE the tomato sauce, heat the olive oil in a saucepan and cook the garlic gently until light brown. Add half the rosemary or thyme and then the tomatoes. Season with salt and pepper and cook gently, stirring occasionally, until reduced to a thick tomato sauce.

PREHEAT the oven to 180°C (350°F/Gas 4). Turn the polenta out of the dish and onto a board, then slice it horizontally in two. Pour half the tomato sauce into the bottom of the empty dish. Place the bottom slice of the polenta on top of the sauce and season. Scatter the Gorgonzola and Taleggio over the top. Dot the mascarpone over the polenta with a teaspoon, and sprinkle with half the Parmesan and the remaining herbs.

PUT the other layer of polenta on top and pour over the remaining tomato sauce. Sprinkle with the remaining Parmesan and bake for 30 minutes. Leave to rest for 10 minutes before serving with a simple rocket salad.

Arrange the first layer of polenta carefully in the dish but don't worry if you break it — it will seal again as it cooks. Lay the cheese in an even layer on top of the polenta before finishing with the final layers.

Risotto rice comes in different types, all varying in absorbency. For this reason cooking times cannot be entirely accurate — just keep stirring until it is done.

At Antica Riseria Ferron in the Veneto, rice is husked by hand then polished to produce perfect white grains.

MILANESE RISOTTO

MILANESE RISOTTO, THE CLASSIC ACCOMPANIMENT TO OSSO BUCO, TAKES ITS BRILLIANT YELLOW COLOUR FROM SAFFRON AND ITS RICH FLAVOUR FROM BEEF MARROW. IF BEEF MARROW IS HARD TO FIND, YOU CAN USE A FATTY PIECE OF LARDO, PROSCIUTTO OR PANCETTA, FINELY CHOPPED.

200 ml dry white vermouth or white wine
large pinch of saffron threads
1.5 litres chicken stock
100 g butter
75 g beef marrow
1 large onion, finely chopped
1 garlic clove, crushed
350 g risotto rice (arborio, vialone nano or carnaroli)
50 g Parmesan, grated

SERVES 6 AS A SIDE DISH

PUT the vermouth in a bowl, add the saffron and leave to soak. Put the stock in a saucepan, bring to the boil and then maintain at a low simmer.

MELT the butter and beef marrow in a large wide heavy-based saucepan. Add the onion and garlic and cook until softened but not browned. Add the rice and reduce the heat to low. Season and stir briefly to thoroughly coat the rice.

ADD the vermouth and saffron to the rice. Increase the heat and cook, stirring, until all the liquid has been absorbed. Stir in a ladleful of the simmering stock and cook over moderate heat, stirring continuously. When the stock has been absorbed, stir in another ladleful. Continue like this for about 20 minutes, until all the stock has been added and the rice is *al dente*. (You may not need to use all the stock, or you may need a little extra—every risotto will be slightly different.)

STIR IN a handful of Parmesan and serve the rest on the side for people to help themselves.

SEAFOOD RISOTTO

AS WITH MOST SEAFOOD DISHES, DON'T SERVE THIS RISOTTO WITH PARMESAN. IN LOMBARDIA AND PIEMONTE, RISOTTO IS CREAMY BUT THE GRAINS RETAIN A 'BITE'. VENETIANS MAKE THEIR RISOTTOS *ALL'ONDA*, ALMOST LIQUID LIKE SOUPS, TO BE EATEN WITH A SPOON. YOU CAN CHOOSE EITHER STYLE.

185 g squid tubes
200 g prawns
4 tablespoons olive oil
2 garlic cloves, crushed
185 g firm white fish fillets, such as monkfish, sea bass or fresh haddock, skinned and cut into bite-sized pieces
16 scallops, cleaned
1 litre fish stock
1 leek, white part only, thinly sliced
350 g risotto rice (arborio, vialone nano or carnaroli)
125 ml dry white wine
3 plum tomatoes, chopped
1 tablespoon butter
1 1/2 tablespoons finely chopped parsley
1 1/2 tablespoons finely chopped dill

SERVES 4

CUT the squid tubes into thinner rings. Peel and devein the prawns.

HEAT HALF the olive oil in a large wide heavy-based saucepan. Add the garlic and cook gently without browning for 20–30 seconds. Add the squid and prawns and season lightly. Increase the heat and cook until they turn opaque. Remove the squid and prawns from the pan and set aside.

ADD the fish and scallops to the pan and cook until the fish and scallops change colour. Remove from the pan and set aside.

PUT the stock in a saucepan, bring to the boil and then maintain at a low simmer.

ADD the remaining olive oil to the large wide pan. Add the leek and cook for 3–4 minutes, or until softened but not browned. Add the rice and reduce the heat to low. Season and stir briefly to thoroughly coat the rice, then add the white wine. Increase the heat and cook, stirring, until all the liquid has been absorbed.

STIR IN a ladleful of the simmering stock and cook over moderate heat, stirring continuously. When the stock has been absorbed, stir in another ladleful. Continue like this for about 20 minutes, until all the stock has been added and the rice is *al dente*. (You may not need to use all the stock, or you may need a little extra—every risotto will be slightly different. If you prefer, add more stock to make the risotto more liquid.) Add the tomato and cooked seafood and toss lightly.

REMOVE the saucepan from the heat and gently stir in the butter and chopped herbs. Season with salt and black pepper. Spoon into warm serving bowls and serve at once.

Cooking the seafood quickly over high heat keeps it tender.

ASPARAGUS RISOTTO

THIS RISOTTO IS PARTICULARLY FLAVOURSOME BECAUSE THE ASPARAGUS STEMS ARE PUREED WITH
THE STOCK AND SO ADDED TO THE RISOTTO DURING THE COOKING. THE ADDITION OF CREAM AT THE
END GIVES A RICH CONSISTENCY.

Gabriele Ferron cooking risotto at
his restaurant in Isola della Scala.

For freshness, grate the Parmesan
from a block as you need it. Take
care as you fold in the asparagus
tips—they break easily.

1 kg asparagus
500 ml chicken stock
500 ml vegetable stock
4 tablespoons olive oil
1 small onion, finely chopped
350 g risotto rice (arborio, vialone
    nano or carnaroli)
75 g Parmesan, grated
3 tablespoons double cream

SERVES 4

WASH the asparagus and remove the woody
ends (hold each spear at both ends and bend it
gently—it will snap at its natural breaking point).
Separate the tender spear tips from the stems.

COOK the asparagus stems in boiling water for
8 minutes, or until very tender. Drain and place in
a blender with the chicken and vegetable stocks.
Blend for 1 minute, then put in a saucepan, bring
to the boil and maintain at a low simmer.

COOK the asparagus tips in boiling water for
1 minute, drain and refresh in iced water.

HEAT the olive oil in a large wide heavy-based
saucepan. Add the onion and cook until softened
but not browned. Add the rice and reduce the
heat to low. Season and stir briefly to thoroughly
coat the rice. Stir in a ladleful of the simmering
stock and cook over moderate heat, stirring
continuously. When the stock has been absorbed,
stir in another ladleful. Continue like this for about
20 minutes, until all the stock has been added
and the rice is *al dente*. (You may not need to use
all the stock, or you may need a little extra—every
risotto will be slightly different.)

ADD the Parmesan and cream and gently stir in
the asparagus tips. Season with salt and pepper
and serve hot.

RED WINE RISOTTO

THE SECRET TO A REALLY SPECTACULAR RED WINE RISOTTO IS TO USE ONLY THE VERY BEST INGREDIENTS. AS THE DISH IS SO SIMPLE, A GOOD-QUALITY WINE IS REQUIRED—TRADITIONALLY THE DRY RICH AMARONE OF VALPOLICELLA IS USED.

500 ml chicken stock
100 g butter
1 onion, finely chopped
1 large garlic clove, crushed
2 tablespoons chopped thyme
225 g risotto rice (arborio, vialone nano or carnaroli)
500 ml dry red wine
50 g Parmesan, grated

SERVES 4 AS A STARTER

PUT the stock in a saucepan, bring to the boil and then maintain at a low simmer.

HEAT the butter in a large wide heavy-based saucepan. Add the onion and garlic and cook until softened but not browned. Add the thyme and rice and reduce the heat to low. Season and stir briefly to thoroughly coat the rice.

ADD HALF the red wine. Increase the heat and cook, stirring, until all the liquid has been absorbed. Stir in a ladleful of the simmering stock and cook over moderate heat, stirring continuously. When the stock has been absorbed, stir in another ladleful. Continue like this for about 10 minutes, until you have added half the stock.

ADD the remaining red wine to the risotto, stirring continuously until it has been absorbed. Stir in another ladleful of the stock and then continue for about 10 minutes until all the stock has been added and the rice is *al dente*. (You may not need to use all the stock, or you may need a little extra—every risotto will be slightly different.)

STIR IN half the Parmesan just before serving with the remaining cheese to be sprinkled on top.

Stir the rice into the butter and onion mixture, making sure that you coat all the grains. Add the red wine and stir continuously so that the rice does not stick to the bottom of the pan and the grains are kept separate.

Adding the wine to the ink and rice helps the ink dissolve and spread evenly through the risotto.

RISOTTO NERO

YOU CAN SOMETIMES BUY THE INK SAC OF THE SQUID FROM YOUR FISHMONGER, ALTHOUGH MOST ARE LOST OR BURST BY THE TIME THE SQUID REACHES THE SHOP. THE LITTLE SACHETS OF INK ARE MORE EASILY FOUND. SQUID INK QUALIFIES AS SEAFOOD, SO DON'T SERVE THIS RISOTTO WITH PARMESAN.

2 medium-sized squid
1 litre fish stock
100 g butter
1 red onion, finely chopped
2 garlic cloves, crushed
350 g risotto rice (arborio, vialone nano or carnaroli)
3 sachets of squid or cuttlefish ink, or the ink sac of a large cuttlefish
150 ml white wine
2 teaspoons olive oil

SERVES 6 AS A STARTER

PREPARE the squid by pulling the heads and tentacles out of the bodies along with any innards. Cut the heads off below the eyes, leaving just the tentacles. Discard the heads and set the tentacles aside. Rinse the bodies, pulling out the transparent quills. Finely chop the bodies.

PUT the stock in a saucepan, bring to the boil and then maintain at a low simmer.

HEAT the butter in a large wide heavy-based saucepan and cook the onion until softened but not browned. Increase the heat and add the chopped squid. Cook for 3–5 minutes, or until the squid turns opaque. Add the garlic and stir briefly. Add the rice and reduce the heat to low. Season and stir briefly to thoroughly coat the rice.

SQUEEZE OUT the ink from the sachets and add to the rice with the wine. Increase the heat and stir until all the liquid has been absorbed.

STIR IN a ladleful of the simmering stock and cook over moderate heat, stirring continuously. When the stock has been absorbed, stir in another ladleful. Continue like this for about 20 minutes, until all the stock has been added and the rice is *al dente*. (You may not need to use all the stock, or you may need a little extra—every risotto will be slightly different.)

HEAT the olive oil in a frying pan and fry the squid tentacles quickly. Garnish the risotto with the tentacles and serve immediately.

MUSHROOM RISOTTO

20 g dried porcini mushrooms
1 litre vegetable or chicken stock
2 tablespoons olive oil
1 tablespoon butter
1 small onion, finely chopped
2 garlic cloves, crushed
375 g risotto rice (arborio, vialone
  nano or carnaroli)
250 g mushrooms, sliced
pinch of nutmeg
45 g Parmesan, grated
3 tablespoons finely chopped
  parsley

SERVES 4

SOAK the porcini in 500 ml boiling water for
30 minutes. Drain, retaining the liquid. Chop the
porcini mushrooms and pass the liquid through a
fine sieve. Put the stock in a saucepan, bring to
the boil and then maintain at a low simmer.

HEAT the olive oil and butter in a large wide
heavy-based saucepan. Cook the onion and garlic
until softened but not browned. Add the rice and
reduce the heat to low. Season and stir briefly to
thoroughly coat the rice. Toss in the fresh
mushrooms and nutmeg. Season and cook,
stirring, for 1–2 minutes. Add the porcini and their
liquid, increase the heat and cook until the liquid
has been absorbed.

STIR IN a ladleful of stock and cook over moderate
heat, stirring continuously. When the stock has
been absorbed, stir in another ladleful. Continue
like this for about 20 minutes, until all the stock
has been added and the rice is *al dente*. (You may
not need to use all the stock, or you may need a
little extra.) Remove from the heat and stir in the
Parmesan and parsley. Season and serve.

Dried porcini give an earthiness
to dishes. When used with fresh
mushrooms they add an attractive
depth of flavour.

RISI E BISI

THE CONSISTENCY OF RISI E BISI IS THICK, HALFWAY BETWEEN A RISOTTO AND A SOUP IN TEXTURE
AND APPEARANCE. YOU CAN COOK IT THIN ENOUGH TO EAT WITH A SPOON, OR THICK ENOUGH TO USE
A FORK. SOME VERSIONS ARE VERY SIMPLE AND DO NOT EVEN INCLUDE PANCETTA.

1.5 litres chicken or vegetable stock
2 teaspoons olive oil
40 g butter
1 small onion, finely chopped
80 g pancetta, cut into small cubes
2 tablespoons chopped parsley
375 g shelled young peas
200 g risotto rice (arborio, vialone
  nano or carnaroli)
50 g Parmesan, grated

SERVES 4

PUT the stock in a saucepan, bring to the boil
and then maintain at a low simmer. Heat the oil
and half the butter in a large wide heavy-based
saucepan and cook the onion and pancetta over
low heat for 5 minutes until softened. Stir in the
parsley and peas and add 2 ladlefuls of the stock.
Simmer for 6–8 minutes.

ADD the rice and the remaining stock. Simmer
until the rice is *al dente* and most of the stock has
been absorbed. Stir in the remaining butter and
the Parmesan, season and serve.

RISI E BISI

ROMAN GNOCCHI

THESE GNOCCHI CAN BE PREPARED A DAY OR TWO IN ADVANCE, WRAPPED AND STORED IN THE REFRIGERATOR IN THE SLAB FORM OR AS CIRCLES. ROMAN GNOCCHI ARE MADE WITH SEMOLINA AND ARE QUITE DIFFERENT FROM THE MORE WELL-KNOWN POTATO GNOCCHI SERVED WITH PASTA SAUCE.

45 g unsalted butter, melted
30 g Parmesan, grated
3 egg yolks
1 litre milk
pinch of nutmeg
200 g semolina flour

TOPPING
40 g butter, melted
90 ml double cream
30 g Parmesan, grated

SERVES 4

A biscuit cutter gives a good clean edge to the gnocchi. If you don't have one, use an upturned glass or teacup instead.

LINE a 30 x 25 cm swiss roll tin with baking paper. Beat together the butter, Parmesan and egg yolks and season lightly. Set aside.

HEAT the milk in a large saucepan. Add the nutmeg, and season with salt and pepper. When the milk is just boiling, pour in the semolina in a steady stream, stirring as you pour. Reduce the heat and continue to cook, stirring, for about 10–12 minutes, or until all the milk has been absorbed and the mixture pulls away from the side of the pan in one mass.

REMOVE the pan from the heat and beat in the egg yolk mixture. When smooth, spoon quickly into the swiss roll tin. Smooth the surface to give an even thickness, using a knife dipped in cold water. Set aside to cool.

PREHEAT the oven to 180°C (350°F/Gas 4) and grease a 25 x 18 cm shallow casserole or baking tray.

LIFT the semolina slab out of the tin and peel off the baking paper. Cut the semolina into circles, using a 4 cm biscuit cutter dipped in cold water. Arrange the circles, slightly overlapping, in the greased casserole.

TO MAKE the topping, blend together the butter and cream. Pour this over the gnocchi and sprinkle the Parmesan on top. Transfer to the oven and bake for about 25–30 minutes, or until golden. Serve at once.

This cheesemaker has just opened a whole Parmesan. Traditionally Parmesan is 'flaked', as shown here, rather than cut.

POTATO GNOCCHI WITH PANCETTA AND SAGE

WHEN COOKING THE POTATOES FOR GNOCCHI YOU WANT TO KEEP THEM AS DRY AS POSSIBLE—TOO MUCH MOISTURE WILL RESULT IN A HEAVY DOUGH. FLOURY POTATOES HAVE A LOW MOISTURE CONTENT AND BAKING THE POTATOES IN THEIR SKINS KEEPS THEM DRIER THAN BOILING.

GNOCCHI
1 kg floury potatoes, unpeeled
2 egg yolks
2 tablespoons grated Parmesan
125–185 g plain flour

SAUCE
1 tablespoon butter
75 g pancetta or bacon, cut into
  thin strips
8 very small sage or basil leaves
150 ml double cream
50 g Parmesan, grated

SERVES 4

PRICK the potatoes all over, then bake for 1 hour, or until tender. Leave to cool for 15 minutes, then peel and mash, or put through a ricer or a food mill (do not use a blender or food processor).

MIX IN the egg yolks and Parmesan, then gradually stir in the flour. When the mixture gets too dry to use a spoon, work with your hands. Once a loose dough forms, transfer to a lightly floured surface and knead gently. Work in enough extra flour to give a soft, pliable dough that is damp to the touch but not sticky.

DIVIDE the dough into six portions. Working with one portion at a time, roll out on the floured surface to make a rope about 1.5 cm thick. Cut the rope into 1.5 cm lengths. Take one piece of dough and press your finger into it to form a concave shape, then roll the outer surface over the tines of a fork to make deep ridges. Fold the outer lips in towards each other to make a hollow in the middle. Continue with the remaining dough.

BRING a large saucepan of salted water to the boil. Add the gnocchi in batches, about 20 at a time. Stir gently and return to the boil. Cook for 1–2 minutes, or until they rise to the surface. Remove them with a slotted spoon, drain and put in a greased shallow casserole or baking tray. Preheat the oven to 200°C (400°F/Gas 6).

TO MAKE the sauce, melt the butter in a small frying pan and fry the pancetta until crisp. Stir in the sage leaves and cream. Season and simmer for 10 minutes, or until thickened.

POUR the sauce over the gnocchi, toss gently and sprinkle the Parmesan on top. Bake for 10–15 minutes, or until the Parmesan melts and turns golden. Serve hot.

Knead enough to just bring the dough together and make it smooth. Keep the work surface, your hands and any storage trays well floured. Roll and shape the dough quickly to stop it drying out.

Fold the filling into the crepes and place them at an angle in the dish, so the filling doesn't run out as it heats up.

CRESPELLE

THE ITALIAN VERSION OF CREPES, THESE PANCAKES ARE VERY POPULAR IN THE SOUTH. THEY CAN BE ROLLED OUT AND USED TO MAKE A CANNELLONI TYPE DISH, OR FOLDED AS HERE. EACH OF THE FILLINGS BELOW MAKES ENOUGH FOR ABOUT 12 CREPES.

CREPES
200 g plain flour
3 eggs
220 ml milk
3–4 tablespoons butter

CHICKEN LIVER, SPINACH AND CHEESE FILLING
1 tablespoon butter
150 g chicken livers, trimmed
pinch of nutmeg
60 g spinach, shredded
220 g ricotta
90 g Parmesan, grated
2 tablespoons chopped parsley
1 quantity tomato sauce (page 285)

HAM, EGG AND ASPARAGUS FILLING
150 g asparagus, chopped
20 g butter
1 tablespoon plain flour
125 ml hot milk
2 tablespoons grated Parmesan
1 teaspoon chopped basil
2 eggs, hard-boiled and chopped
120 g ham, cut into strips
50 g melted butter
75 g Parmesan, grated

MAKES 12 CREPES

TO MAKE the crepes, place the flour in a bowl. Make a well in the centre and add the eggs and a good pinch of salt. Mix well with a wooden spoon. Gradually pour in the milk combined with 185 ml water, whisking constantly until you have a smooth runny batter. Leave to rest for 2 hours.

STIR the batter and add a little more water, if necessary, to return it to the original consistency. Heat a little butter in an 18 cm crepe pan. Spoon in 2–3 tablespoons of batter, tilting the pan to cover the base. Cook for 1 minute, until brown but not set, then turn over with a spatula and cook for another 30 seconds until set. Slide onto a plate and cook the rest of the batter. Preheat the oven to 180°C (350°F/Gas 4).

TO MAKE the chicken liver, spinach and cheese filling, heat the butter in a saucepan and cook the chicken livers for 3 minutes. Season with salt, pepper and the nutmeg and finely chop. Put the spinach in the pan and cook until wilted. Mash the ricotta with a fork and add the Parmesan. Stir in the parsley, chicken livers and spinach, and season. Place a spoonful of filling in the centre of each crepe and roll up, or fold it in half and then half again. Place in a greased shallow ovenproof dish, pour the tomato sauce over the top and bake for 20 minutes.

TO MAKE the ham, egg and asparagus filling, simmer the asparagus in boiling salted water for 3 minutes. Melt the butter in a saucepan, stir in the flour, then add the hot milk, stirring until you have a thick sauce. Stir in the Parmesan, basil, eggs, asparagus and ham, and season well. Place a spoonful of filling in the centre of each crepe and roll up, or fold it in half and then half again. Place in a greased shallow ovenproof dish or baking tray, sprinkle the melted butter and Parmesan on top and bake for 20 minutes.

CRESPELLE WITH CHICKEN LIVER, SPINACH AND CHEESE FILLING

CRESPELLE WITH HAM, EGG AND ASPARAGUS FILLING

MAKING PASTA SECCA Pastificio Faella, near Naples, is owned by Signore Mario Faella and is one of the few pastificios (artisan pasta factories) to still use the traditional methods for making pasta. Italian farmers cannot grow enough wheat to meet demand, so a fine-grade (00) Italian durum wheat semolina (*Pasta di Semola di Grano Duro*) is mixed with drier imported flour and water to create *pasta alimentare*. The high amount

PASTA

PASTA WAS ORIGINALLY A SOUTHERN ITALIAN, PARTICULARLY SICILIAN, DISH, WITH THE FIRST PASTA INDUSTRY LOCATED IN NAPLES TO TAKE ADVANTAGE OF ITS PURE WATER, LOCAL GRAIN AND ABUNDANT SUNSHINE.

It was Mussolini who moved the cultivation of wheat, and therefore pasta, to other areas of Italy, and emigrating Italians who made it famous throughout the world. Nowadays, northern Italy tends to eat fresh egg and filled pastas (*pasta fresca*), often with rich meat or cream sauces or sometimes with just melted butter and Parmesan. Emilia-Romagna in the North now rivals Naples as the centre of pasta production, with its fresh pasta made daily by hand. The

South specializes in dried durum wheat semolina pasta made without egg (*pasta secca*). The hard durum wheat is needed to form the pasta into shapes and also to maintain its *al dente* consistency. This dried pasta is usually eaten with less rich and vegetable sauces. In Italy, pasta tends to be eaten as a *primo piatti*, or first course, rather than as a main course, and is always cooked fresh to order.

TYPES OF PASTA SECCA (DRIED PASTA)

PASTA CORTA short shapes, from the tiny ones used in soups to the familiar penne, farfalle and fusilli. Many of these pastas are hollow so that they cook evenly.

PASTA LUNGA long shapes such as spaghetti and tagliatelle, or any variety over about 10 cm.

PASTA ALL'UOVO SECCA this dried egg pasta is made from a combination of durum wheat semolina and eggs and can only be made by machine because of the toughness of the dough. The shapes vary from ribbons, sold in nests, to filled pasta shapes such as tortellini or ravioli.

MAKING PASTA FRESCA The chefs at Borgo San Felice, Tuscany, make fresh pasta daily, just as many other restaurants in Italy do. Fresh pasta is made using a soft wheat 00 (*doppio zero*) flour and free-range eggs, rather than the harder durum wheat semolina used for making dried pasta. The flour and eggs are poured into the top of the pasta machine, which mixes the dough before extruding it through variously

of protein in the grain means there is no need for any other binding agents and it allows the pasta to pass easily through a die (the traditional brass die makes a whiter pasta with a roughness that helps the pasta pick up sauce). As the pasta passes through the die, it is shaped and cut to length, then dried slowly on trays in hot rooms. Finally, it is packaged up and sold by weight from the small shop in front of the factory.

TYPES OF PASTA FRESCA (FRESH PASTA)

PASTA FRESCA ALL'UOVO made from eggs and a soft wheat 00 flour, this pasta is eaten mostly in the North and can be moulded easily into shapes such as tortellini and cappelletti, as well as being rolled out to make sheets of lasagne and pasta ribbons.

PASTA DI SEMOLA FRESCA unlike fresh pasta from the North, this home-made pasta from the South is created from just durum wheat semolina and water. The most common shapes are fusilli, orecchiette and strozzapreti.

MATCHING SAUCES TO PASTA

Pastas are crafted to complement certain sauces. Shapes are often available as *lisci* (smooth) and *rigati* (ridged) and should be served with just enough sauce to coat them. The drained cooking water from the pasta can be added to the sauce if it is too thick.

SMALL PASTA SHAPES (alfabeto, ditalini, orzo and stelline) known as *pastina,* these pastas are added to soups. There are many different shapes, ranging from letters and numbers to stars, rings and tiny shells.

LONG PASTA (trenette, linguine, spaghetti, bucatini, ziti) best eaten with fine-textured sauces such as pesto, tomato sauce or a meat ragù that will cling to their lengths. They are also used in *pasticcios*.

PASTA RIBBONS (tagliatelle, fettuccine) serve with simple, fresh flavourings such as truffles or with creamy mushroom or ham sauces. When yellow and green ribbons are served together they are known as 'straw and hay'.

PASTA SHAPES (fusilli, lumache, orecchiette) serve with thicker, chunkier sauces, which are trapped by their shape. Pasta shapes also go well with sauces that have pieces of sausage, seafood or vegetable in them or with thicker soup-like dishes such as *pasta e fagioli*.

STUFFED PASTAS (cappelletti, tortelli, ravioli) as they already have flavoured fillings such as meat, pumpkin or spinach, filled pastas go well with simple sauces such as butter and sage, a fresh tomato sauce or in a *pasta in brodo*.

sized dies. As the pasta passes through the machine, lengths of it are cut and laid out to dry on a tray that has been sprinkled with semolina to stop it sticking. More semolina is sprinkled on as the layers build up, before the whole batch is tossed together to coat it. The same pasta dough is also rolled out thin and cut into sheets for lasagne or used to make filled pastas such as tortellini and ravioli.

SPAGHETTI CARBONARA

THE ORIGIN OF THIS DISH IS HOTLY DISPUTED. WAS IT BROUGHT TO ROME BY THE *CARBONARI* (COAL MEN) FROM UMBRIA? OR INSPIRED BY THE EGG AND BACON RATIONS OF THE AMERICAN GI'S? OR PERHAPS NAMED AFTER THE NINETEENTH CENTURY RADICAL GROUP, *I CARBONARI*?

400 g spaghetti
2 eggs
2 egg yolks
60 g Parmesan, grated, plus extra
   for serving
2 tablespoons olive oil
30 g butter
2 garlic cloves
200 g pancetta, cut into small strips

SERVES 4

COOK the pasta in a large saucepan of boiling salted water until *al dente*. Meanwhile, mix the eggs, egg yolks and Parmesan together in a bowl and season lightly.

HEAT the oil and butter in a large frying pan. Bruise the garlic cloves with the back of a knife and add to the pan with the pancetta. Cook over moderate heat until the pancetta is crisp, discarding the garlic when it becomes golden.

DRAIN the spaghetti, add to the frying pan and toss well. Remove from the heat and stir in the egg mixture. Serve immediately, with Parmesan.

SPAGHETTI CARBONARA

TAGLIATELLE WITH WALNUT SAUCE

200 g shelled walnuts
20 g roughly chopped parsley
50 g butter
200 ml extra virgin olive oil
1 garlic clove, crushed
30 g Parmesan, grated
100 ml double cream
400 g pasta, such as tagliatelle

SERVES 4

LIGHTLY TOAST the walnuts in a dry frying pan over moderately high heat for 2 minutes, or until browned. Set aside to cool for 5 minutes.

PUT the walnuts in a food processor with the parsley and blend until finely chopped. Add the butter and mix together.

GRADUALLY pour in the olive oil in a steady stream with the motor running. Add the garlic, Parmesan and the cream. Season with salt and black pepper.

COOK the pasta in a large saucepan of boiling salted water until *al dente*. Drain, then toss through the sauce to serve.

Walnuts grow all over Italy, with the best coming from Campania and Liguria. Green walnuts are used to make a *digestif* called *nocino*.

TAGLIATELLE WITH TRUFFLES

IF YOU ARE GOING TO THE EXTRAVAGANCE OF USING TRUFFLES, DON'T SKIMP ON THE PARMESAN—USE PARMIGIANO REGGIANO FOR THE BEST FLAVOUR. IF YOU CAN'T GET A FRESH TRUFFLE, USE ONE FROM A JAR, PRESERVED IN BRINE.

135 g butter
1 garlic clove
400 g fresh tagliatelle
60 g Parmesan, grated
1 small white Alba truffle or black
  Norcia truffle

SERVES 4 AS A STARTER

MELT the butter in a saucepan over moderately low heat. Add the garlic clove and heat until the butter bubbles, separates and turns lightly golden. Strain the butter.

MEANWHILE, cook the pasta in a large saucepan of boiling salted water until *al dente*. Drain and return to the saucepan. Add the browned butter and the Parmesan. Season with salt and black pepper and toss lightly.

PLACE ON warmed plates and take to the table. Using a mandolin or potato peeler, shave a few very thin slices of the truffle onto each serving.

Black truffles are found around Norcia in Umbria. When they're not in season, use preserved truffles.

SPAGHETTI VONGOLE

2 tablespoons olive oil
3 cloves garlic, crushed
2 pinches of chilli flakes
1 teaspoon chopped parsley
125 ml dry white wine
2 x 400 g tins chopped tomatoes
1 kg clams
3 tablespoons finely chopped
  parsley
400 g spaghetti or linguine
1/2 teaspoon grated lemon zest
lemon wedges

SERVES 4

HEAT the oil in a large deep frying pan. Add the garlic and chilli and cook over low heat for 30 seconds. Add the parsley, wine and tomatoes. Increase the heat and boil, stirring occasionally, for 8–10 minutes until the liquid is reduced by half.

CLEAN the clams by scrubbing them thoroughly. Rinse well under running water. Discard any that are broken or cracked or do not close when tapped on the work surface. Add to the saucepan. Cover the pan, increase the heat and cook for 3–5 minutes until the clams open. Shake the pan often. Remove the clams from the pan, discarding any that stay closed. Stir in the parsley and season. Uncover the pan and boil until thick. Set 12 clams aside and extract the meat from the rest.

COOK the pasta in a large saucepan of boiling salted water until *al dente*. Drain and stir through the sauce. Add the lemon zest, reserved clams and clam meat and toss well. Serve with the lemon wedges.

SPAGHETTI VONGOLE

PASTA WITH BORLOTTI BEANS

200 g dried borlotti beans
2 tablespoons olive oil
100 g pancetta, diced
1 celery stalk, chopped
1 onion, finely chopped
1 carrot, diced
1 garlic clove, crushed
3 tablespoons chopped parsley
1 bay leaf
400 g tin chopped tomatoes,
   drained
1.5 litres vegetable stock
150 g ditalini or macaroni
drizzle of extra virgin olive oil
grated Parmesan

SERVES 4

PLACE the beans in a large saucepan, cover with cold water and soak overnight. Drain and rinse under cold water.

HEAT the olive oil in a large saucepan and add the pancetta, celery, onion, carrot and garlic and cook over moderately low heat for 5 minutes until golden. Season with black pepper. Add the parsley, bay leaf, tomatoes, stock and borlotti beans and bring slowly to the boil. Reduce the heat and simmer for 1–1½ hours, or until the beans are tender, adding a little boiling water every so often to maintain the level.

ADD the pasta and simmer for about 6 minutes, or until the pasta is just *al dente*. Remove from the heat and leave to rest for 10 minutes. Serve warm with a drizzle of extra virgin olive oil over each bowl. Serve the Parmesan separately.

Chickpeas are grown in the south of Italy but appear in the cuisines of all regions, either whole or ground into *farinata* (flour).

PASTA WITH CHICKPEAS

250 g dried chickpeas
3 tablespoons olive oil
1 large onion, finely chopped
1 celery stalk, finely chopped
1 carrot, finely chopped
2 garlic cloves, crushed
1 rosemary sprig
pinch of crushed dried chilli
2 tablespoons tomato purée
1.5 litres vegetable stock
125 g small pasta shells
drizzle of extra virgin olive oil
grated Parmesan

SERVES 4

PUT the chickpeas in a large saucepan, cover with cold water and soak overnight. Drain and rinse under cold water.

HEAT the olive oil in a large saucepan, add the chopped vegetables, garlic and rosemary and cook over moderately low heat for 8 minutes. Add the chilli and season. Stir in the tomato purée and stock, then add the chickpeas. Bring to the boil. Reduce the heat and simmer for 1–1½ hours, or until the chickpeas are tender, adding a little boiling water every so often to maintain the level.

ADD the pasta and continue cooking until it is *al dente*. Remove the rosemary sprig. Drizzle with extra virgin olive oil and sprinkle with Parmesan.

PASTA WITH CHICKPEAS

Speciality pastas are still produced by small family firms, using old-fashioned methods and bronze dies for shaping.

PASTA PRIMAVERA

PASTA (MEANING 'DOUGH' IN ITALIAN, FROM THE SAME ROOT AS 'PASTRY' AND THE FRENCH 'PATE') HAS A LONG HISTORY AND WAS PROBABLY ENJOYED BY BOTH THE ANCIENT GREEKS AND ETRUSCANS. THIS FAVOURITE SAUCE, WITH ITS FRESH YOUNG VEGETABLES, HERALDS THE ARRIVAL OF SPRINGTIME.

120 g broad beans, fresh or frozen
150 g asparagus, cut into short
  lengths
350 g fresh tagliatelle
100 g French beans, cut into short
  lengths
120 g peas, fresh or frozen
30 g butter
1 small fennel bulb, thinly sliced
375 ml double cream
2 tablespoons grated Parmesan,
  plus extra to serve

SERVES 4

BRING a large saucepan of water to the boil. Add 1 teaspoon of salt, the broad beans and the asparagus and simmer for 3 minutes.

REMOVE the vegetables with a slotted spoon and set aside. Add the tagliatelle to the saucepan and, when it has softened, stir in the French beans and the peas (if you're using frozen peas add them a few minutes later). Cook for about 4 minutes, or until the pasta is *al dente*.

MEANWHILE, heat the butter in a large frying pan. Add the fennel and cook over moderately low heat without colouring for 5 minutes. Add the cream, season with salt and pepper and cook at a low simmer.

PEEL the skins from the broad beans. Drain the pasta, French beans and peas and add to the frying pan. Add 2 tablespoons of Parmesan and the broad beans and asparagus. Toss lightly to coat. Serve immediately, with extra Parmesan.

TOMATO AND
RICOTTA ORECCHIETTE

TOMATO AND RICOTTA ORECCHIETTE

400 g orecchiette
470 g plum tomatoes
315 g ricotta
45 g Parmesan, grated,
  plus extra to serve
8 basil leaves, torn into pieces

SERVES 4

COOK the pasta in a large saucepan of boiling salted water until *al dente*.

SCORE a cross in the top of each tomato, plunge them into boiling water (you can use the pasta water) for 20 seconds, then drain and peel the skin away from the cross. Core and chop. Mash the ricotta, add the Parmesan and season.

DRAIN the pasta and return to the pan. Add the ricotta mixture, the tomato and basil. Season and toss. Serve at once, with Parmesan.

TAGLIATELLE WITH RAGU

SPAGHETTI BOLOGNESE IS ONE OF THE MOST POPULAR AND WELL-KNOWN ITALIAN DISHES AROUND THE WORLD. HOWEVER, THE ITALIANS THEMSELVES WOULD NEVER DREAM OF SERVING THEIR TRADITIONAL BOLOGNESE SAUCE ON SPAGHETTI—TAGLIATELLE IS THE USUAL ACCOMPANIMENT.

60 g butter
1 onion, finely chopped
1 celery stalk, finely chopped
1 carrot, finely chopped
90 g pancetta or bacon, finely
  chopped
220 g minced beef
220 g minced pork
2 oregano sprigs, chopped, or
  1/4 teaspoon dried oregano
pinch of nutmeg
120 g chicken livers, trimmed and
  finely chopped
125 ml dry white wine
215 ml milk
400 g tin chopped tomatoes
250 ml beef stock
400 g tagliatelle
grated Parmesan

SERVES 4

HEAT the butter in a saucepan and add the onion, celery, carrot and pancetta. Cook over moderate heat for 6–8 minutes, stirring from time to time.

ADD the minced beef, pork and oregano to the saucepan. Season with salt and pepper and the nutmeg. Cook for about 5 minutes, or until the mince has changed colour but not browned. Add the chicken liver and cook until it changes colour.

POUR IN the wine, increase the heat and boil over high heat for 2 3 minutes, or until the wine has been absorbed. Stir in 125 ml of the milk, reduce the heat and simmer for 10 minutes. Add the tomatoes and half the stock, partially cover the pan and leave to simmer gently over very low heat for 3 hours. Add more of the stock as it is needed to keep the sauce moist.

MEANWHILE, cook the pasta in a large saucepan of boiling salted water until al dente. Stir the remaining milk into the sauce 5 minutes before serving. Taste the sauce for seasoning, then drain the tagliatelle, toss with the sauce and serve with grated Parmesan.

The backstreets of Bologna.

SPAGHETTINI AGLIO E OLIO

400 g spaghettini
90 ml olive oil
5 garlic cloves, crushed
pinch of dried chilli flakes
2 tablespoons finely chopped
  parsley
grated pecorino

SERVES 4

COOK the pasta in a large saucepan of boiling salted water until *al dente*.

MEANWHILE, heat the oil in a large frying pan over very low heat. Add the garlic and chilli flakes and gently fry for about 2 minutes, or until the garlic has softened but not browned. Remove the frying pan from the heat.

LIGHTLY DRAIN the spaghettini. Don't shake it dry in the colander, as you need it to retain a little of the cooking water. Return the frying pan to the heat, add the spaghettini and parsley and toss to coat. Taste for seasoning and serve at once with the grated pecorino.

Growing olives that will later be pressed into olive oil.

PENNE ALL'ARRABBIATA

BECAUSE THERE IS CHILLI IN THE SAUCE, DON'T SERVE WITH PARMESAN—JUST A DRIZZLE OF GOOD-QUALITY EXTRA VIRGIN OLIVE OIL. THE CHILLI IS WHAT GIVES THIS DISH ITS NAME: 'ANGRY SAUCE'. GOOD-TASTING FRESH TOMATOES CAN BE USED INSTEAD OF THE TINNED, BUT PEEL THEM FIRST.

2 tablespoons olive oil
2 large garlic cloves, thinly sliced
1–2 medium-sized dried chillies
800 g tin tomatoes
400 g penne or rigatoni
1 basil sprig, torn into pieces

SERVES 4

HEAT the olive oil in a saucepan and add the garlic and chillies. Cook over low heat until the garlic is light golden brown. Turn the chillies over during cooking so both sides get a chance to infuse in the oil and turn slightly nutty in flavour. Add the tomatoes and season with salt. Cook gently, breaking up the tomatoes with a wooden spoon, for about 20–30 minutes, or until the sauce is rich and thick.

MEANWHILE, cook the pasta in a large saucepan of boiling salted water until *al dente*. Drain.

ADD the basil to the sauce and season just before serving, tossed with the pasta. If you prefer a hotter sauce, break open the chilli to release the seeds.

PENNE ALL'ARRABBIATA

PASTA IN BRODO

DIFFERENT PASTAS CAN BE SERVED *IN BRODO* (BROTH). TORTELLINI IN BRODO IS OFTEN SERVED AS THE *PRIMO PIATTO* AT CELEBRATIONS. AT OTHER TIMES, ANY PLAINER PASTA IS USED WITH VEGETABLES FOR A SIMPLE SOUP.

BROTH
2 tablespoons olive oil
1 large onion, chopped
2 carrots, chopped
1 celery stalk, chopped
1.5 kg chicken bones
4 large garlic cloves, unpeeled
1 bay leaf
small bunch of parsley stalks and
   thyme sprigs
1 large wine glass of red or white
   wine

24 fresh tortellini or some large
   ravioli (wild mushroom or meat
   stuffings are particularly good)
grated Parmesan
3 tablespoons roughly chopped
   flat-leaf parsley

SERVES 6

TO MAKE the broth, heat the olive oil in a saucepan and lightly brown the onion, carrot and celery. Add the chicken bones and lightly brown (this will give a good flavour to your broth). Add the garlic, herbs and wine, cook for a few minutes to reduce, then add enough water to completely cover the bones. Bring slowly to the boil, skimming the top several times to get rid of any scum that rises to the surface of the broth.

GENTLY SIMMER the broth for at least 1 hour. Strain through a fine sieve, pour the broth back into a saucepan and return to the heat. Cook until the broth has reduced a little (this will give it a more concentrated, gutsy flavour). Taste the broth and remove from the heat when you feel the flavour is strong enough. This should produce about 1.35 litres of flavoursome broth.

FOR a clearer broth, leave to chill in the fridge overnight, then scrape the fat and sediment from the surface and pour off the broth, leaving the sediment behind.

(UP TO this point, the broth can be made in advance and can be frozen for a few months—any longer and the flavour will start to diminish.)

COOK the pasta in a large saucepan of boiling salted water until *al dente.* Meanwhile, heat the broth in another saucepan (don't be tempted to cook the pasta in the broth—the semolina used to prevent home-made pasta sticking can spoil the flavour). Drain the pasta well and add to the heated broth. Remove from the heat and leave to infuse for a couple of minutes, then spoon the pasta into bowls and pour over the broth. Sprinkle with Parmesan and the parsley to serve.

Use the largest pot you have to make the broth so the bones and vegetables are fully covered with liquid. A conical sieve is easier to use for draining as it directs the liquid through in one stream. For a clear broth make sure the mesh is fine enough to collect all the bits.

SPAGHETTI WITH PRAWNS, CLAMS AND SCALLOPS

SEAFOOD PASTA IN MANY RESTAURANTS AROUND THE WORLD IS ERRONEOUSLY TERMED *MARINARA*. MARINARA IS TRADITIONALLY THE SAUCE MADE BY FISHERMEN (OR THEIR WIVES), TO WHICH THE DAY'S CATCH WOULD BE ADDED. SO THE NAME, IN FACT, REFERS TO THE SAUCE, NOT THE SEAFOOD.

The prawns, squid and octopus are added first as they take marginally longer to cook than the scallops and clams.

250 ml dry white wine
pinch of saffron threads
1 kg clams
4 baby octopus
200 g small squid tubes
500 g prawns
6 tomatoes
400 g spaghetti
4 tablespoons olive oil
3 garlic cloves, crushed
8–10 scallops, cleaned
6 tablespoons chopped parsley
lemon wedges

SERVES 4

PUT the wine and saffron in a bowl and leave to infuse. Clean the clams by scrubbing them thoroughly and scraping off any barnacles. Rinse well under running water and discard any that are broken or open and don't close when tapped on the work surface. Place them in a large saucepan with 185 ml water. Cover the pan and cook over high heat for 1–2 minutes, or until they open (discard any that stay closed after that time). Drain, reserving the liquid. Remove the clams from their shells and set aside.

CLEAN the octopus by slitting the head and pulling out the innards. Cut out the eyes and hard beak and rinse. Lie the squid out flat, skin side up, and score a criss-cross pattern into the flesh, being careful not to cut all the way through. Slice diagonally into 2 x 4 cm strips. Peel and devein the prawns.

SCORE a cross in the top of each tomato, plunge them into boiling water for 20 seconds, then drain and peel the skin away from the cross. Core and chop. Cook the pasta in a large saucepan of boiling salted water until *al dente*.

MEANWHILE, heat the oil in a large frying pan and add the garlic and tomato. Stir over moderate heat for 10–15 seconds, then pour in the saffron-infused wine and the reserved clam liquid. Season and simmer for 8–10 minutes, or until reduced by half. Add the squid, prawns and octopus and cook until the squid turns opaque. Add the scallops, clam meat and parsley and cook until the scallops turn opaque.

DRAIN the spaghetti and return to the pan. Add two-thirds of the sauce, toss well then transfer to a large serving platter. Spoon the remaining sauce over the top and serve with lemon wedges.

SPAGHETTI ALLA PUTTANESCA

4 tablespoons olive oil
1 small onion, finely chopped
2 garlic cloves, finely sliced
1 small red chilli, cored, seeded and sliced
6 anchovy fillets, finely chopped
400 g tin chopped tomatoes
1 tablespoon finely chopped oregano or 1/4 teaspoon dried oregano
100 g pitted black olives, halved
1 tablespoon capers, chopped if large
400 g spaghetti

SERVES 4

HEAT the olive oil in a large saucepan and add the onion, garlic and chilli. Fry gently for about 6 minutes, or until the onion is soft. Add the anchovies and cook, stirring, until well mixed.

ADD the tomatoes, oregano, olives and capers and bring to the boil. Reduce the heat, season and leave to simmer.

MEANWHILE, cook the pasta in a large saucepan of boiling salted water until *al dente*. Drain, toss well with the sauce and serve at once.

BUCATINI ALL'AMATRICIANA

A SPECIALITY OF THE LAZIO REGION, ESPECIALLY THE TOWN OF AMATRICE AFTER WHICH IT IS NAMED. THIS DISH IS TRADITIONALLY MADE WITH GUANCIALE, CURED PIG'S CHEEK, BUT PANCETTA IS AN ACCEPTABLE SUBSTITUTE. PECORINO CAN BE USED INSTEAD OF PARMESAN.

1 tablespoon olive oil
150 g guanciale or pancetta, in 2 thick slices
1 small onion, finely chopped
2 garlic cloves, crushed
3/4 teaspoon dried chilli flakes
600 g tin chopped tomatoes
400 g bucatini
2 tablespoons finely chopped parsley
grated Parmesan

SERVES 4

HEAT the oil in a large saucepan. Trim the fat from the pancetta and add the fat to the pan. Cook the pancetta fat over medium-high heat until it is crisp to extract the liquid fat, then discard the rinds. Dice the pancetta, add to the saucepan and cook until lightly browned.

ADD the onion and fry gently for about 6 minutes, or until soft. Add the garlic and chilli flakes and cook, stirring, for 15–20 seconds then stir in the tomatoes. Season with salt and pepper.

SIMMER the sauce for about 15 minutes, or until it thickens and darkens.

MEANWHILE, cook the pasta in a large saucepan of boiling salted water until *al dente*. Stir the parsley into the sauce, drain the pasta, toss together well and serve with Parmesan.

BUCATINI ALL'AMATRICIANA

RAVIOLI APERTO

FILLING
30 g butter
1 small onion, finely chopped
85 g baby spinach leaves
250 g ricotta
3 tablespoons double cream

1 quantity pasta (page 278),
   rolled out
100 g frozen spinach, thawed
250 ml chicken stock

SERVES 4

TO MAKE the filling, melt the butter in a frying pan and add the onion. Cook, stirring, for 5 minutes, or until softened. Add the baby spinach leaves and cook for 4 minutes. Remove from the heat, cool to room temperature and then chop. Add the ricotta and 2 tablespoons of the cream and stir well. Season with salt and pepper.

TO MAKE the ravioli, cut the rolled out pasta into sixteen 8 cm squares and cook in a large saucepan of boiling salted water until *al dente*. Drain. Preheat the oven to 180°C (350°F/Gas 4).

LINE a baking tray with baking parchment and lay out half the pieces of pasta on the tray. Divide the filling into eight portions and spoon into the centre of each square. Place the other eight pasta sheets on top to enclose the filling and cover with a damp tea towel.

TO MAKE a sauce, blend the spinach with a little of the chicken stock until smooth. Transfer to a saucepan with the remaining stock and heat for 2 minutes. Add the remaining cream, stir well, season and remove from the heat.

HEAT the ravioli in the oven for 5 minutes, or until just warm. Place two ravioli on each plate, reheat the sauce gently, pour over the ravioli and serve immediately.

Take time to place the filling carefully in the middle of each pasta square, so it doesn't ooze out of the sides when it cooks.

PIZZOCCHERI

THIS BUCKWHEAT PASTA IS A CLASSIC RECIPE FROM VALTELLINA NEAR THE SWISS BORDER AND USES THE MOST COMMON FOODS OF THAT AREA. IT IS BEST EATEN AFTER STRENUOUS EXERCISE IN THE FRESH AIR—THIS IS QUITE A STURDY DISH.

PIZZOCCHERI
200 g buckwheat flour
100 g plain bread flour
1 egg
120 ml milk, warmed

CHEESE, POTATO AND
CABBAGE SAUCE
350 g savoy cabbage or any other
   cabbage, roughly chopped
180 g potatoes, cubed
4 tablespoons olive oil
1 tablespoon chopped sage
2 garlic cloves, crushed
350 g Italian cheeses, such as
   fontina or Taleggio, cubed
75 g Parmesan, grated

SERVES 4

TO MAKE the pizzoccheri, sift the two flours into a bowl and add a pinch of salt. Make a well in the centre and add the egg. Mix the egg into the flour and then gradually add the milk, mixing continuously until you have a soft dough (you may need more or less milk, depending on the dryness of your flour).

KNEAD the dough for a few minutes, or until it is elastic, and then cover it with a tea towel and leave to rest for an hour. Using a pasta machine or a rolling pin, roll out the dough very thinly and cut into noodles about 1 cm wide.

TO MAKE the sauce, bring a large saucepan of salted water to the boil. Add the cabbage and potato and cook for about 3–5 minutes or until they are cooked through. Add the pizzoccheri and cook for a further 2 minutes. Drain, reserving a cup of the cooking water.

HEAT the oil in a saucepan and gently cook the sage and garlic for 1 minute. Add the cheese cubes and mix briefly, then add the cabbage, potato and pizzoccheri and season with salt and pepper. Remove from the heat and gently stir the mixture together, adding some pasta water to loosen it a little. Serve immediately with the Parmesan sprinkled on top.

ALTERNATIVELY, if you prefer your cheese completely melted, spoon everything into a casserole dish and heat in the oven for 5 minutes.

TORTELLINI FILLED WITH PUMPKIN AND SAGE

LEGEND HAS IT THAT VENUS, BARRED FROM HEAVEN, SOUGHT REFUGE IN AN INN IN BOLOGNA INSTEAD. THE INNKEEPER, FILLED WITH LUST, SPIED ON HER THROUGH THE KEYHOLE, THEN RUSHED TO HIS KITCHEN TO CREATE PASTA IN THE SHAPE OF HER NAVEL—TORTELLINI.

Brushing the pasta with egg wash will make sure it holds together when filled and shaped. Don't overfill the tortellini or the filling will ooze out as it cooks. Pinching the edges together on the fat side of the pasta makes tortellini. Pinching them away from the fat side makes cappelletti (bishops' hats).

FILLING
900 g pumpkin or butternut squash, peeled and cubed
6 tablespoons olive oil
1 small red onion, finely chopped
100 g ricotta
1 egg yolk, beaten
25 g Parmesan, grated
1 teaspoon grated nutmeg
2 tablespoons chopped sage

1 quantity pasta (page 278), rolled out
1 egg
2 teaspoons milk

SAGE BUTTER
250 g butter
10 g sage leaves

grated Parmesan

SERVES 6

TO MAKE the filling, preheat the oven to 190°C (375°F/Gas 5). Put the pumpkin in a roasting tin with half the olive oil and lots of salt and pepper. Bake in the oven for 40 minutes, or until it is completely soft.

MEANWHILE, heat the remaining olive oil in a saucepan and gently cook the onion until soft. Put the onion and pumpkin in a bowl, draining off any excess oil, and mash well. Leave to cool, then crumble in the ricotta. Mix in the egg yolk, Parmesan, nutmeg and sage. Season well.

TO MAKE the tortellini, cut the rolled out pasta into 8 cm squares. Mix together the egg and milk to make an egg wash and brush lightly over the pasta just before you fill each one. Put a small teaspoon of filling in the middle of each square and fold it over diagonally to make a triangle, pressing down the corners. Pinch together the two corners on the longer side.

(IF YOU are not using the tortellini immediately, place them, well spaced out, on baking paper dusted with cornmeal and cover with a tea towel. They can be left for 1–2 hours before cooking— don't refrigerate or they will become damp.)

COOK the tortellini, in small batches, in a large saucepan of boiling salted water until *al dente*. Remove and drain with a slotted spoon.

TO MAKE the sage butter, melt the butter slowly with the sage and leave to infuse for at least 5 minutes. Drizzle over the tortellini and serve with a sprinkling of Parmesan.

RAVIOLI

FILLING
30 g butter
1/2 small onion, finely chopped
2 garlic cloves, crushed
90 g prosciutto, finely chopped
125 g finely minced pork
125 g finely minced veal
1/2 teaspoon finely chopped fresh
   oregano, or 1/8 teaspoon dried
   oregano
1 teaspoon paprika
1/2 tablespoon tomato purée
125 ml chicken stock
2 egg yolks

1 quantity pasta (page 278),
   rolled out
semolina
1 egg, beaten

SERVES 4

TO MAKE the filling, heat the butter in a frying pan. Cook the onion, garlic and prosciutto over moderately low heat for 5–6 minutes without browning. Add the pork and veal, increase the heat and lightly brown, breaking up the lumps. Add the oregano and paprika, season well and stir in the tomato purée and chicken stock.

COVER the pan and cook for 50 minutes. Uncover, increase the heat and cook for another 10 minutes until the filling is quite dry. Cool, then chop to get rid of any lumps. Stir in the egg yolks.

TO MAKE the ravioli, divide the rolled out pasta into four sheets: two 30 x 20 cm sheets and two slightly larger. Dust the work surface with semolina and lay out one of the smaller sheets (keep the rest of the pasta covered with a damp tea towel to prevent it drying out). Lightly score the pasta sheet into 24 squares. Place a scant teaspoon of filling in the centre of each square and flatten it slightly with the back of the spoon.

BRUSH beaten egg along the score lines around the filling. Take one of the larger pasta sheets and cover the first, starting at one end. Match the edges and press the top sheet onto the beaten egg as you go. Avoid stretching the top sheet, rather let it settle into place. Run your finger firmly around the filling and along the cutting lines to seal well. Use a pastry wheel or sharp knife to cut into 24 ravioli squares.

(IF YOU are not using the ravioli immediately, place them, well spaced out, on baking paper dusted with cornmeal and cover with a tea towel. They can be left for 1–2 hours before cooking — don't refrigerate or they will become damp.)

Cook the ravioli, in small batches, in a large saucepan of boiling salted water until *al dente*. Remove and drain with a slotted spoon. Serve on their own or with melted butter, a drizzle of olive oil or grated Parmesan.

Making ravioli by scoring the pasta, adding the filling, covering it and then cutting it is much easier than cutting the pasta fiirst. You can also use a special fluted ravioli wheel to cut the edges, giving a crimped effect.

The steep streets of Naples.

Layer the meat, pasta and cheese in the pastry, smoothing the layers to keep them even.

PASTICCIO OF MACARONI AND RAGU

PASTICCIO IS A GENERIC TERM IN THE ITALIAN KITCHEN, MEANING A PIE MADE UP OF VARIOUS LAYERS. THE PREPARATION IS TIME-CONSUMING, SO PASTICCIO IS OFTEN A SPECIAL OCCASION DISH. IT CAN BE MADE WITH A PASTRY CRUST OR WITHOUT, BUT THESE DAYS IT ALWAYS TENDS TO CONTAIN PASTA.

FILLING
2 tablespoons butter
1 tablespoon olive oil
1 onion, finely chopped
2 garlic cloves, crushed
500 g minced beef
60 g button mushrooms, finely
   sliced
115 g chicken livers, trimmed and
   finely chopped
pinch of nutmeg
1 tablespoon dry Marsala
3 tablespoons dry white wine
2 tablespoons tomato purée
250 ml chicken stock
3 tablespoons grated Parmesan
1 egg

PASTRY
300 g plain flour
2 teaspoons caster sugar
100 g butter, cubed
1 egg
about 2 tablespoons chilled water

150 g macaroni
100 g ricotta
50 g Parmesan, grated
2 tablespoons milk
pinch of cayenne pepper
1 egg, beaten
120 g mozzarella, grated

SERVES 6

TO MAKE the filling, heat the butter and oil in a large frying pan and cook the onion and garlic over moderate heat for 5–6 minutes until golden. Add the beef, increase the heat and cook until browned, breaking up any lumps.

ADD the mushrooms, livers and nutmeg, season and cook until the livers change colour. Add the Marsala and wine and cook until they evaporate. Stir in the purée and stock, reduce the heat and simmer for 30 minutes. Remove from the heat and season. Beat the Parmesan and egg together and quickly stir through the meat.

TO MAKE the pastry, sift the flour, sugar and 1 teaspoon salt into a bowl and rub in the butter. Add the egg and the cold water, a little at a time, stirring until the dough comes together. Transfer to a lightly floured board and knead lightly until smooth. Put in a plastic bag and refrigerate.

COOK the macaroni in a large saucepan of boiling salted water until *al dente,* then drain. Meanwhile, blend together the ricotta, Parmesan, milk, cayenne and half the egg. Season well and stir in the macaroni. Preheat the oven to 180°C (350°F/Gas 4) and grease a deep-sided pie dish.

DIVIDE the pastry into two balls, one larger than the other. On a lightly floured work surface, roll out the larger ball to line the dish with overlapping edges. Roll out the second ball large enough to cover the pie dish. Spread half the filling into the pastry-lined pie dish, then layer half the pasta over it. Top with half the mozzarella. Repeat the layers.

BRUSH the pie rim with beaten egg and cover with the pastry lid. Brush the top with egg and make three slits in the centre with a sharp knife. Bake for 50 minutes, until golden, and leave to rest for 10 minutes before serving.

PASTICCIO OF TORTELLINI, BROCCOLI AND RICOTTA

FILLING
650 g ricotta
pinch of nutmeg
90 g Parmesan, grated
1 egg

600 g broccoli, trimmed into florets
500 g cheese-filled tortellini
3 eggs
1 quantity béchamel sauce (page 285)
1 1/2 tablespoons tomato purée
150 g mozzarella, grated
4 tablespoons grated Parmesan

SERVES 6

TO MAKE the filling, mash the ricotta with a fork, or pass through a food mill (do not use a blender or food processor). Mix in the nutmeg and salt and pepper. Add the Parmesan, then mix in the egg. Set aside.

PREHEAT the oven to 180°C (350°F/Gas 4) and grease a large deep casserole dish. Bring a large saucepan of water to the boil. Add the broccoli florets and a teaspoon of salt and simmer for 3 minutes. Remove the broccoli with a slotted spoon and set aside. Stir the tortellini into the boiling water and then gently lower in the eggs. Cook until the pasta is *al dente*, drain and rinse under cold water. Take out the eggs when they have had 6 minutes and are hard-boiled, remove the eggshells and slice thinly.

PUT HALF of the béchamel sauce into a large bowl and stir in the tomato purée. Add the tortellini and toss to coat. Pour half of this mixture into the casserole dish. Spread half of the ricotta filling over it, then top with half the egg slices. Layer all the broccoli on top of this, pressing it in firmly, then spoon the remaining plain béchamel sauce over the top. Sprinkle with the mozzarella. Finish with a final layer of tortellini, the remaining egg slices and finally the rest of the ricotta filling.

SPRINKLE the Parmesan over the top and bake for 30–40 minutes. Remove from the oven and allow to rest for 10 minutes before serving.

Ricotta is made from the whey left over from cheese-making. These ricotta are made from the whey of Parmesan cheese.

Bakeries and speciality shops make pasta daily. Here, tortellini and caramelle are made at Paolo Atti e Figli bakery in Bologna.

LASAGNE AL FORNO

MEAT SAUCE
30 g butter
1 onion, finely chopped
1 small carrot, finely chopped
1/2 celery stalk, finely chopped
1 garlic clove, crushed
120 g pancetta, sliced
500 g minced beef
1/4 teaspoon dried oregano
pinch of nutmeg
90 g chicken livers, trimmed and
    finely chopped
75 ml dry vermouth or dry white
    wine
350 ml beef stock
1 tablespoon tomato purée
2 tablespoons double cream
1 egg, beaten

1 quantity béchamel sauce (page
    285)
125 ml double cream
100 g fresh lasagne verde or
    6 sheets dried lasagne
150 g mozzarella, grated
60 g Parmesan, grated

SERVES 6

Lasagne is traditionally made with lasagne verde. Make sure the layers fit without overlapping too much or the lasagne will be stodgy. Leave enough béchamel for a good thick layer on top.

TO MAKE the meat sauce, heat the butter in a frying pan and add the chopped vegetables, garlic and pancetta. Cook over moderately low heat for 5–6 minutes, or until softened and lightly golden. Add the minced beef, increase the heat a little and cook for 8 minutes, or until coloured but not browned, stirring to break up the lumps. Add the oregano and nutmeg and season well.

STIR IN the chicken livers and cook until they change colour. Pour in the vermouth, increase the heat and cook until it has evaporated. Add the beef stock and tomato purée and simmer for 2 hours. Add a little hot water, if necessary, during this time to keep the mixture moist, but towards the end let all the liquid be absorbed. Stir in the cream, remove from the heat and leave to cool for 15 minutes. Stir in the egg.

PUT the béchamel in a saucepan, heat gently and stir in the cream. Remove from the heat and cool slightly. Preheat the oven to 180°C (350°F/Gas 4) and grease a 22 x 15 x 7 cm ovenproof dish.

IF YOU are using fresh pasta, cut it into manageable sheets and cook in batches in a large saucepan of boiling salted water until *al dente*. Scoop out each batch with a slotted spoon as it is done and drop into a bowl of cold water. Spread the sheets out in a single layer on a tea towel, turning them over once to blot dry each side. Trim away any torn edges.

SPREAD HALF the meat sauce in the dish. Scatter with half the mozzarella, then cover with a slightly overlapping layer of pasta sheets. Spread half the béchamel over this and sprinkle with half the Parmesan. Repeat the layers, finishing with a layer of béchamel and Parmesan.

BAKE for about 40 minutes until golden brown and leave to rest for 10 minutes before serving.

VINCISGRASSI

MEAT SAUCE
40 g butter
2 cotechino sausages, casings
    removed, chopped
800 g chicken thigh fillets, cut into
    thin strips
300 g chicken livers, trimmed and
    chopped
75 ml dry Marsala
200 ml chicken stock

MUSHROOM SAUCE
10 g dried porcini mushrooms
40 g butter
1 onion, finely chopped
100 g button mushrooms,
    finely sliced
pinch of nutmeg
1 tablespoon chicken stock

1½ quantities béchamel sauce
    (page 285)
100 g fresh lasagne or 6 sheets
    dried lasagne
75 g Parmesan, grated

SERVES 6

TO MAKE the meat sauce, heat the butter in a large frying pan and cook the sausage meat until browned, stirring to break up any lumps. Add the chicken and lightly brown. Increase the heat, add the liver and fry quickly, stirring, until darkened. Season, pour in the Marsala and stir until almost evaporated, then add the stock. Cover, reduce the heat and simmer for 25 minutes.

TO MAKE the mushroom sauce, soak the dried porcini in 75 ml warm water for 30 minutes. Drain and finely chop the porcini. Heat the butter in a saucepan and soften the onion over low heat for 5–6 minutes. Add the porcini and button mushrooms and cook over high heat for 2–3 minutes. Add the nutmeg and chicken stock. Season and simmer for 8–10 minutes, or until all the liquid has evaporated.

POUR ONE THIRD of the béchamel sauce into a bowl and refrigerate. Add the mushroom sauce to the remaining béchamel and mix well.

IF YOU are using fresh pasta, cook in batches in a large saucepan of boiling salted water until *al dente*. Scoop out each batch with a slotted spoon and drop into a bowl of cold water. Spread the sheets out in a single layer on a tea towel, turning them over once to blot dry each side. Trim away any torn edges.

GREASE a large ovenproof dish and make an overlapping layer of pasta in the base. Top with half the meat sauce, then spread half of the mushroom sauce over the top. Sprinkle with one third of the Parmesan. Repeat the layers, then finish with a layer of pasta. Refrigerate the last of the Parmesan. Cover the vincisgrassi with clingfilm and refrigerate for at least 6 hours.

PREHEAT the oven to 200°C (400°F/Gas 6). Spoon the reserved béchamel sauce over the top and sprinkle the remaining Parmesan over this. Bake for 30 minutes, or until golden, and rest for 10 minutes before serving.

Grease the dish and line with pasta before spooning in the meat and mushroom sauces.

CANNELLONI

Roll the pasta around the filling fairly tightly, then lay the cannelloni seam side down in the dish.

MEAT SAUCE
3 tablespoons olive oil
1 onion, finely chopped
2 garlic cloves, crushed
120 g bacon, finely chopped
60 g button mushrooms, finely
  chopped
1/4 teaspoon dried basil
220 g minced pork
220 g minced veal
1 tablespoon finely chopped parsley
200 g tin chopped tomatoes
250 ml beef stock
3 tablespoons dried breadcrumbs
1 egg

TOMATO SAUCE
2 tablespoons olive oil
1 small onion, finely chopped
2 garlic cloves, crushed
2 x 400 g tins chopped tomatoes
1 teaspoon chopped basil

10 sheets fresh lasagne, about
  17 x 12 cm (the grain of the pasta
  should run with the width not the
  length, or the pasta will split when
  rolled up), or 1 1/2 quantities pasta
  (page 278) rolled and cut into
  10 sheets as above
4 large slices prosciutto, cut in half
60 g fontina, grated
200 ml double cream
60 g Parmesan, grated

SERVES 4

TO MAKE the meat sauce, heat the oil in a frying pan and cook the onion, garlic and bacon over moderate heat for 6 minutes, or until the onion is soft and golden. Stir in the mushrooms and basil, cook for 2–3 minutes, then add the pork and veal. Cook, stirring often to break up the lumps, until the mince has changed colour. Season well, add the parsley, tomatoes and stock, partially cover the pan and simmer for 1 hour. Remove the lid and simmer for another 30 minutes to reduce the liquid. Cool slightly then stir in the breadcrumbs, then the egg.

TO MAKE the tomato sauce, heat the oil in a frying pan and cook the onion and garlic for 6 minutes, or until the onion has softened but not browned. Stir in the tomatoes and basil. Add 250 ml water and season well. Simmer for 30 minutes, or until you have a thick sauce.

COOK the lasagne in batches in a large saucepan of boiling salted water until al dente. Scoop out each batch with a slotted spoon and drop into a bowl of cold water. Spread the sheets out in a single layer on a tea towel, turning them over once to blot dry each side. Trim away any torn edges. (We have allowed two extra sheets of fresh lasagne in case of tearing.)

PREHEAT the oven to 190°C (375°F/Gas 5). Grease a shallow 30 x 18 cm ovenproof dish and spoon the tomato sauce over the base.

PLACE a half slice of prosciutto over each pasta sheet. Top with a sprinkling of fontina. Spoon an eighth of the meat filling across one end of the pasta sheet. Starting from this end, roll the pasta up tightly to enclose the filling. Place the filled rolls, seam side down, in a row in the dish.

BEAT TOGETHER the cream and Parmesan and season well. Spoon over the cannelloni so that it is covered. Bake for 20 minutes, or until lightly browned on top. Leave to rest for 10 minutes before serving.

TIMBALLO

THE ELABORATE BAKED PIES OF RENAISSANCE ITALY, CALLED *PASTICCI* OR *TORTE,* WERE EMBRACED BY FRENCH CUISINE AND RENAMED *TIMBALES.* TWO CENTURIES LATER, THE ITALIANS RECLAIMED THE TIMBALE AS THEIR OWN AND IT WAS CHRISTENED THE TIMBALLO.

6 tomatoes
2 tablespoons olive oil
1 large onion, finely chopped
2 garlic cloves, crushed
5 chicken breast fillets
4 chicken thighs
1 bay leaf
2 thyme sprigs
3 tablespoons white wine
175 g mushrooms, sliced
75 g provolone, grated
9 eggs, beaten
2 tablespoons double cream
3 tablespoons chopped parsley
800 g ziti

SERVES 6

SCORE a cross in the top of each tomato, plunge into boiling water for 20 seconds, then drain and peel the skin away from the cross. Dice the flesh.

HEAT the oil in a large saucepan, add the onion and garlic and cook, stirring, for 7 minutes or until softened. Add the tomato and cook for 5 minutes over low heat. Add the chicken breasts and thighs, the bay leaf and thyme and stir well. Add the wine, cover the pan and cook over moderate heat for 20 minutes.

ADD the mushrooms to the saucepan and cook for another 10–15 minutes, turning the chicken once or twice until it is cooked through. Remove the chicken from the saucepan and cook the sauce until it has reduced and thickened. Remove the bay leaf and thyme and leave the sauce to cool to room temperature.

REMOVE the chicken meat from the bones, shred the meat and return to the sauce. Stir in the cheese, eggs, cream and parsley. Season with salt and pepper.

PREHEAT the oven to 180°C (350°F/Gas 4) and grease a round 1.25 litre ovenproof dish with a little butter or oil.

COOK the pasta in a large saucepan of boiling salted water until *al dente*. Drain well and place in the dish, one by one, in a single layer, starting in the middle and spiralling outwards to cover the base and side. Make sure there are no gaps.

FILL the centre with the chicken sauce and bake for 1 hour. Leave to rest for a few minutes, then invert onto a plate to serve.

Start coiling the ziti in the centre of the base and work your way to the outer edge. Then build up the side, without leaving any gaps.

DESSERTS & BAKING

TIRAMISU

TIRA MI SU MEANS 'PICK ME UP' IN ITALIAN AND THIS IS HOW THE DESSERT STARTED LIFE—AS A NOURISHING DISH TO BE EATEN WHEN FEELING LOW. YOU CAN ALSO MAKE A FRUIT VERSION, USING FRAMBOISE AND PUREED RASPBERRIES INSTEAD OF BRANDY AND COFFEE.

5 eggs, separated
180 g caster sugar
300 g mascarpone
250 ml cold strong coffee
3 tablespoons brandy or sweet
  Marsala
36 small sponge fingers
80 g dark chocolate, finely grated

SERVES 4

BEAT the egg yolks with the sugar until the sugar has dissolved and the mixture is light and fluffy and leaves a ribbon trail when dropped from the whisk. Add the mascarpone and beat until the mixture is smooth.

WHISK the egg whites in a clean dry glass bowl, using a wire whisk or hand beaters, until soft peaks form. Fold into the mascarpone mixture.

POUR the coffee into a shallow dish and add the brandy. Dip enough biscuits to cover the base of a 25 cm square dish into the coffee. The biscuits should be fairly well soaked but not so much so that they break up. Arrange the biscuits in one tightly packed layer in the base of the dish.

SPREAD half the mascarpone mixture over the layer of biscuits. Add another layer of soaked biscuits and then another layer of mascarpone, smoothing the top layer neatly. Dust with the grated chocolate to serve. The flavours will be better developed if you can make the tiramisu a few hours in advance or even the night before. If you have time to do this, don't dust with the chocolate, but cover with clingfilm and chill. Dust with chocolate at the last minute or it will melt.

Made from cream rather than milk and a speciality of southern Lombardia, mascarpone is usually found as an ingredient in dishes rather than eaten as a cheese.

PANNA COTTA

MEANING 'COOKED CREAM', THIS PIEMONTESE DESSERT SHOULD BE SOFTLY SET WITH A YELLOW COLOUR AND A RICH CREAMY TEXTURE. DON'T BE TEMPTED TO PUT ANY MORE GELATINE IN THE MIXTURE OR YOUR PANNA COTTA MIGHT BECOME RUBBERY.

450 ml double cream
4 tablespoons caster sugar
vanilla extract
3 sheets or 1 1/4 teaspoons gelatine
250 g fresh berries

SERVES 4

PUT the cream and sugar in a saucepan and stir over gentle heat until the sugar has dissolved. Bring to the boil, then simmer for 3 minutes, adding a few drops of vanilla extract to taste.

IF YOU are using the gelatine sheets, soak in cold water until they are floppy, then squeeze out any excess water. Stir the sheets into the hot cream until they are completely dissolved. If you are using powdered gelatine, sprinkle it onto the hot cream in an even layer and leave it to sponge for a minute, then stir it into the cream until dissolved.

POUR the cream mixture into four 125 ml dariole moulds, cover each with a piece of clingfilm and refrigerate until set.

UNMOULD the panna cotta by wrapping the moulds in a cloth dipped in hot water and tipping them gently onto individual plates. Serve with the fresh berries.

STRAWBERRIES WITH BALSAMIC VINEGAR

DURING THEIR SEASON, WILD STRAWBERRIES ARE ABUNDANT THROUGHOUT ITALY. AN ACIDIC DRESSING OF CITRUS JUICE OR RED WINE LIFTS BOTH THEIR FLAVOUR AND AROMA. IN EMILIA-ROMAGNA THEY HAVE BEEN SERVED WITH BALSAMIC VINEGAR SINCE RENAISSANCE TIMES.

500 g strawberries, hulled and
   halved
60 ml good-quality balsamic vinegar
2 tablespoons caster sugar
2 teaspoons lemon juice
1/4 cup small mint leaves

SERVES 6

PLACE the strawberries in a glass bowl. Heat the balsamic vinegar, caster sugar and lemon juice in a small saucepan, stirring until combined. Remove from the heat and leave to cool.

POUR the balsamic vinegar over the strawberries, add the mint leaves and toss together. Cover with clingfilm and marinate in the fridge for at least 1 hour. Delicious served over vanilla ice cream.

STRAWBERRIES WITH
BALSAMIC VINEGAR

BAKED PEACHES

THE PEACH IS ONE OF ITALY'S FAVOURITE FRUITS, WITH THE BEST BEING PRODUCED IN LE MARCHE, EMILIA-ROMAGNA AND CAMPANIA. THIS RECIPE ALSO WORKS WELL WITH FRESH APRICOTS. ALLOW THREE APRICOTS PER PERSON.

4 ripe peaches
45 g amaretti biscuits
1 tablespoon sweet Marsala
20 g ground almonds
1 egg yolk
1 tablespoon sugar
25 g unsalted butter
icing sugar

SERVES 4

PREHEAT the oven to 180°C (350°F/Gas 4). Halve the peaches and remove the stones. Crush the amaretti biscuits in a food processor or with the end of a rolling pin and mix them with the Marsala, almonds, egg yolk and sugar.

FILL the peaches with the biscuit mixture, spreading the filling in an even layer over the entire surface. Dot each peach with butter and arrange in a shallow ovenproof dish or baking tray. Bake for 20–30 minutes or until the peaches are tender right through. Dust lightly with icing sugar before serving.

ZABAIONE

ZABAIONE IS ONE OF THOSE HAPPY OCCURRENCES, A DISH CREATED PURELY BY ACCIDENT WHEN, IN SEVENTEENTH CENTURY TURIN, A CHEF POURED FORTIFIED SWEET WINE INTO EGG CUSTARD. IN RURAL AREAS ZABAIONE (ALSO KNOWN AS ZABAGLIONE) IS EATEN HOT FOR BREAKFAST.

6 egg yolks
3 tablespoons caster sugar
125 ml sweet Marsala
250 ml double cream

SERVES 4

WHISK the egg yolks and sugar together in the top of a double boiler or in a heatproof bowl set over a saucepan of simmering water. When the mixture is tepid, add the Marsala and whisk for another 5 minutes, or until it has thickened.

WHIP the cream until soft peaks form. Gently fold in the egg yolk mixture. Cover and refrigerate for 3–4 hours before serving.

ZABAIONE

CASSATA

THERE ARE TWO DIFFERENT DISHES NAMED CASSATA, ONE A CAKE MADE WITH RICOTTA AND CANDIED FRUIT, THE OTHER AN ICE-CREAM DESSERT. THIS CASSATA IN ITS CAKE FORM IS A CLASSIC SICILIAN DISH DECORATED WITH BRIGHTLY COLOURED ICINGS, MARZIPAN AND CANDIED FRUIT.

400 g Madeira or pound cake
4 tablespoons sweet Marsala
350 g ricotta
110 g caster sugar
½ teaspoon vanilla extract
150 g mixed candied fruit (orange, lemon, cherries, pineapple, apricot), chopped
50 g dark chocolate, chopped
green food colouring
200 g marzipan
2 tablespoons apricot jam
300 g icing sugar

MAKES ONE 20 CM CAKE

LINE a 20 cm round cake tin with sloping sides (a *moule à manqué* would be perfect) with clingfilm. Cut the cake into thin slices to line the tin, reserving enough pieces to cover the top at the end. Fit the slices of cake carefully into the tin, making sure there are no gaps. Sprinkle the Marsala over the cake in the tin.

PUT the ricotta in a bowl and beat until smooth. Add the sugar and vanilla extract and mix well. Add the candied fruit and chocolate and mix well. Spoon into the mould, smooth the surface and then cover with the reserved slices of cake. Cover with clingfilm and press the top down hard. Put the cassata in the fridge for at least two hours or preferably overnight, then unmould onto a plate.

KNEAD enough green food colouring into the marzipan to colour it light green. Roll out the marzipan in a circle until it is large enough to completely cover the cassata. Melt the jam in a saucepan with a tablespoon of water and brush over the cassata. Lift the marzipan over the top and trim it to fit around the edge.

MIX the icing sugar with a little hot water to make a smooth icing that will spread easily. Either pipe the icing onto the cassata in a decorative pattern, or drizzle it over the top in a crosshatch pattern.

The pieces of cake need to be fitted into the mould as neatly as possible. Cut smaller pieces of cake to fill any gaps. Sprinkle the Marsala over the cake evenly so no one patch gets too moist. Fill the mould with ricotta and smooth any air bubbles as you go.

ZUCCOTTO

ZUCCOTTO IS A SPECIALITY OF THE CITY OF FLORENCE—ITS SHAPE PERHAPS INSPIRED BY THE ROUNDED ROOF OF THE LOCAL *DUOMO*. ZUCCOTTO IS ALSO A VARIANT OF *ZUCCHETTO*, THE NAME OF THE CARDINALS' SKULL-CAPS.

300 g Madeira or pound cake
3 tablespoons maraschino liqueur
3 tablespoons brandy
500 ml double cream
100 g icing sugar
150 g dark chocolate, roughly chopped
50 g blanched almonds
25 g skinned hazelnuts
25 g candied peel, chopped
cocoa powder, to dust
icing sugar, to dust

SERVES 6

CUT the cake into 1 cm slices and then cut each slice into two triangles. Combine the maraschino and brandy and sprinkle them over the cake.

LINE a round 1.5 litre bowl with a layer of clingfilm and then with the cake slices. Arrange the slices with the narrow point of each triangle pointing into the bottom of the bowl to form a star pattern, fitting each piece snugly against the others so you don't have any gaps. Cut smaller triangles to fit the gaps along the top and keep the rest of the cake for the top.

WHIP the cream until soft peaks form and then whisk in the icing sugar until you have a stiff mixture. Add about a third of the chocolate and the almonds, hazelnuts and candied peel. Mix together thoroughly, then fill the cake-lined bowl with half the mixture, making a hollow in the middle and drawing the mixture up the sides. Leave in the fridge.

MELT the rest of the chocolate in a heatproof bowl over a saucepan of simmering water, or in a microwave, and fold it into the remaining cream mixture. Spoon this into the bowl and then cover the top with a layer of cake triangles, leaving no gaps. Cover the bowl with clingfilm and refrigerate overnight.

TO SERVE, unmould the zuccotto and use a triangular piece of cardboard as a template to dust the top with alternating segments of cocoa and icing sugar.

When filling the zuccotto, try not to disturb the pieces of cake you have arranged. The easiest way is to smooth the filling up the side and then fill the middle afterwards.

LEMON GELATO

GELATO IS THE ITALIAN NAME FOR AN ICE CREAM BASED ON AN EGG CUSTARD MIXTURE, THOUGH IT HAS NOW COME TO MEAN ALL ICE CREAMS, INCLUDING SORBETS. ITALIANS ARE DISCERNING ABOUT ICE CREAM AND FLAVOURS TEND TO BE FRESH AND AROMATIC, OFTEN BASED ON FRUIT.

5 egg yolks
125 g sugar
500 ml milk
2 tablespoons grated lemon zest
185 ml lemon juice
3 tablespoons double cream

SERVES 6

WHISK the egg yolks and half the sugar together until pale and creamy. Place the milk, lemon zest and remaining sugar in a saucepan and bring to the boil. Pour over the egg mixture and whisk to combine. Pour the custard back into the saucepan and cook over low heat, stirring continuously until the mixture is thick enough to coat the back of a wooden spoon—do not allow the custard to boil.

STRAIN the custard into a bowl, add the lemon juice and cream and then cool over ice. Churn in an ice-cream maker following the manufacturer's instructions. Alternatively, pour into a plastic freezer box, cover and freeze. Stir every 30 minutes with a whisk during freezing to break up the ice crystals and give a better texture. Keep in the freezer until ready to serve.

COFFEE GELATO

5 egg yolks
125 g sugar
500 ml milk
120 ml freshly made espresso
1 tablespoon Tia Maria

SERVES 6

WHISK the egg yolks and half the sugar together until pale and creamy. Place the milk, coffee and remaining sugar in a saucepan and bring to the boil. Pour over the egg mixture and whisk to combine. Pour back into the saucepan and cook over low heat, stirring continuously until the mixture is thick enough to coat the back of a wooden spoon—do not allow the custard to boil.

STRAIN the custard into a bowl and cool over ice. Stir in the Tia Maria. Churn in an ice-cream maker following the manufacturer's instructions. Alternatively, pour into a plastic freezer box, cover and freeze. Stir every 30 minutes with a whisk during freezing to break up the ice crystals and give a better texture. Keep in the freezer until ready to serve.

COFFEE GELATO

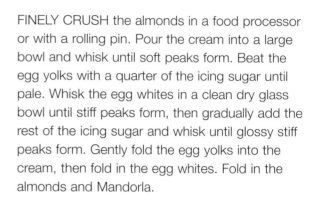

PRALINE SEMIFREDDO

150 g croccante (praline)
600 ml double cream
2 eggs, separated
100 g icing sugar
2 tablespoons Mandorla (almond-
    flavoured Marsala) or brandy

SERVES 6

FINELY CRUSH the almonds in a food processor or with a rolling pin. Pour the cream into a large bowl and whisk until soft peaks form. Beat the egg yolks with a quarter of the icing sugar until pale. Whisk the egg whites in a clean dry glass bowl until stiff peaks form, then gradually add the rest of the icing sugar and whisk until glossy stiff peaks form. Gently fold the egg yolks into the cream, then fold in the egg whites. Fold in the almonds and Mandorla.

LINE six 250 ml metal dariole moulds with two long strips of foil each. Spoon in the mixture, level the surface and tap each mould on the bench a few times. Cover the surface with more foil and freeze for at least 24 hours. To unmould, leave at room temperature for 5 minutes, then use the foil strips as handles to lift out the semifreddos. Serve with zabaione (page 246).

CHOCOLATE SEMIFREDDO

500 ml double cream
150 g caster sugar
50 g cocoa powder
4 eggs, separated
3 tablespoons brandy
3 tablespoons icing sugar
150 g skinned hazelnuts, roughly
    chopped

SERVES 10

LINE a 1.5 litre loaf tin with two long strips of foil. Heat 200 ml of the cream in a small saucepan. Combine the caster sugar, cocoa powder and egg yolks in a bowl. Pour the hot cream on top and mix well. Pour back into the saucepan and cook over low heat, stirring continuously, until the mixture is thick enough to coat the back of a wooden spoon—do not allow the custard to boil. Stir in the brandy and remove from the heat. Cover the surface with clingfilm and cool for 30 minutes.

WHIP the egg whites in a clean dry glass bowl until stiff peaks form. Whip the remaining cream in a large bowl until soft peaks form. Add the icing sugar and continue whipping until stiff and glossy. Lightly fold the chocolate custard into the whipped cream, then fold in the egg whites. Gently fold through the hazelnuts. Spoon into the tin, smooth the surface and cover with foil. Freeze for at least 24 hours. Leave at room temperature for 5 minutes before serving in slices.

CHOCOLATE SEMIFREDDO

RASPBERRY SORBET

SORBETS ARE ICE CREAMS WITHOUT CREAM OR MILK. IF YOU FREEZE A SORBET MIXTURE WITHOUT CHURNING OR WHISKING YOU CAN MAKE A GRANITA—THE ICE CRYSTALS ARE BROKEN UP WITH A FORK INSTEAD FOR A ROUGHER TEXTURE.

125 g sugar
1 tablespoon liquid glucose or
   caster sugar
1/4 teaspoon lemon juice
200 g raspberries

SERVES 4

HEAT the sugar, glucose, lemon juice and 250 ml water in a small saucepan for 4 minutes or until dissolved. Purée the raspberries in a blender or food processor or by mashing with the back of a spoon, add the syrup and process until puréed. Pass through a nylon sieve to remove the seeds.

CHURN in an ice-cream maker following the manufacturer's instructions. Alternatively, pour into a plastic freezer box, cover and freeze. Stir every 30 minutes with a whisk during freezing to break up the ice crystals and give a better texture. Keep in the freezer until ready to serve.

WATERMELON GRANITA

450 g watermelon, rind and seeds
   removed
1 tablespoon liquid glucose or
   caster sugar
1/2 teaspoon lemon juice

SERVES 4

PUREE the watermelon in a blender or food processor, or chop it finely and push it through a metal sieve. Heat the glucose, lemon juice and 75 ml water in a small saucepan for 4 minutes or until dissolved. Add the watermelon and stir well.

POUR into a plastic freezer box, cover and freeze. Stir every 30 minutes with a fork during freezing to break up the ice crystals and give a better texture. Keep in the freezer until ready to serve, then roughly fork to break up the ice crystals.

WATERMELON GRANITA

CAFFE FLORIAN in Venice's Piazza San Marco was established in 1720 and modelled on the coffee houses of Constantinople, which were 'schools of wisdom' for academics and literary figures. Set in a square ringed on three sides by cafés and once described by Napoleon as the Drawing Room of Europe, many of the world's most famous figures have taken coffee at Florian's while discussing art, literature and

COFFEE

FOR A COUNTRY THAT DOESN'T ACTUALLY PRODUCE COFFEE, THIS DRINK IS INCREDIBLY IMPORTANT TO ITALIAN CULTURE. ITALIANS INSIST THEIR COFFEE IS PREPARED PROPERLY, AND THE RITUALS OF MAKING A GOOD ESPRESSO AND OF CAFE LIFE ARE AS IMPORTANT AS THE DRINK ITSELF.

Coffee was first brought to Italy in the sixteenth century by the Arabs. By the seventeenth century, Venice had become the gateway through which the drink spread into Europe, and it was here that the beans were roasted before being dispersed throughout the Continent. As a result of the trade, coffee shops sprang up in Venice for people to enjoy this new drink and the most famous, Caffè Florian, has survived up to this day.

COFFEE BLENDS

The best Italian coffee is made just from high-quality arabica beans, though some brands may be a blend of arabica and the less delicate robusta beans. For the roast, Italians tend to prefer a dark, almost burnt, roast. This gives a very concentrated flavour and aroma and many Italians balance out the edge of bitterness by adding sugar. Surprisingly, the darker the roast, the less caffeine, as caffeine is lost during the roasting process. Italian coffee made in bars in fact has very little caffeine, as not only does it use dark beans but also the making process is so short that the water does not come into contact with the coffee grounds for very long.

politics. Today, this historic coffee house still retains its stylish elegance. Patrons of the café can sit on chairs stretching outside into the square, sip their cappuccinos and watch the world go by to music from the live orchestra. In winter, people can choose instead to settle inside on one of the plush banquettes to enjoy their espressos or perhaps a grappa or Campari from the bar.

MAKING ESPRESSO

To make a coffee, the beans are freshly ground and very hot water is forced through measured amounts of this ground coffee under pressure. This produces the basic espresso—a small amount of coffee topped with a foamy brown *crema*, which can then have milk added to make a cappuccino, latte or macchiato.

In Italy, coffee is drunk in a bar (also known as a caffè bar). People visit for a cappuccino and *cornetto* (a croissant-shaped pastry) on their way to work, or pop in for a quick espresso pick-me-up in the mid-morning or afternoon, all of which are cheaper if taken standing at the bar. In Italy, ordering a *caffè* will always mean you get an espresso. Coffee made at home is usually made in an espresso pot or *moka*, a double jug that boils water and forces it through the coffee grounds under pressure.

Choose pears that have a nice rounded shape and arrange them so they fit neatly against each other in the tart.

FRESH PEAR TART

PASTRY

150 g plain flour
60 g caster sugar
1 teaspoon grated lemon zest
60 g unsalted butter, chilled and cut into small cubes
1 egg yolk

MASCARPONE CREAM

125 g mascarpone
60 g caster sugar
1 egg
$1/4$ teaspoon vanilla extract
1 tablespoon plain flour
2–3 tablespoons milk, as necessary

4 ripe pears
juice of $1/2$ lemon
45 g roasted hazelnuts, roughly chopped
$1^1/2$ tablespoons caster sugar
1 tablespoon apricot jam
1 teaspoon pear liqueur, or other fruit-flavoured liqueur

SERVES 6

TO MAKE the pastry, mix the flour, sugar, lemon zest and a pinch of salt in a bowl. Rub in the butter, then add the egg yolk and 2–3 teaspoons cold water and mix until the dough gathers in a loose clump. Transfer to a lightly floured surface and knead until smooth, adding more flour if needed. Chill in a plastic bag for 30 minutes.

PREHEAT the oven to 190°C (375°F/Gas 5) and grease a 23 cm loose-bottomed tart tin. Lightly dust the work surface with flour and roll the pastry out until large enough to fit the tin. Line the tin neatly, trimming the pastry edges with a knife. Cover the pastry with greaseproof paper and fill with pie weights or uncooked rice or beans. Bake blind for 15 minutes then allow to cool. Reduce the oven to 170°C (325°F/Gas 3).

TO MAKE the mascarpone cream, blend the mascarpone, sugar, egg, vanilla extract and flour together until smooth (you can also use a food processor). Add a little milk if necessary to make the cream spreadable. Spoon the mascarpone cream into the pastry shell and smooth the surface.

PEEL, HALVE and core the pears, brushing the cut surfaces with lemon juice as you prepare each one. Arrange the pear halves like wheel spokes in the tart shell, with the wide base of each pear half to the outside. You may need to trim the last couple so they fit snugly. Place a round piece of pear in the centre. Scatter the hazelnuts over the pears, then sprinkle the sugar over the top. Bake for 45 minutes, or until golden and set and the pears are soft.

HEAT the apricot jam and liqueur in a small saucepan with 2 tablespoons water. Simmer, stirring, for 3–4 minutes until the jam has melted. Strain and brush over the pears. Serve the tart warm or at room temperature.

CANNOLI

IDEALLY YOU SHOULD USE METAL CANNOLI TUBES FOR THIS RECIPE. YOU'LL FIND THESE IN MAJOR DEPARTMENT STORES AND SPECIALITY KITCHEN SHOPS. ALTERNATIVELY, YOU COULD USE 2 CM-WIDE WOODEN OR CANE DOWELING, CUT INTO 12 CM LENGTHS.

PASTRY

150 g plain flour
2 teaspoons cocoa powder
1 teaspoon instant coffee
1 tablespoon caster sugar
20 g unsalted butter, chilled and cut into small cubes
3 tablespoons dry white wine
1 teaspoon dry Marsala

1 egg, beaten
oil for deep-frying

FILLING

300 g ricotta
150 g caster sugar
1/4 teaspoon vanilla extract
1/2 teaspoon grated lemon zest
1 tablespoon candied peel, finely chopped
6 glacé cherries, chopped
15 g dark chocolate, grated
icing sugar

SERVES 6

TO MAKE the pastry, mix the flour, cocoa powder, coffee and sugar in a bowl. Rub in the butter, then add the wine and Marsala and mix until the dough gathers in a loose clump. Transfer to a lightly floured surface and knead until smooth (the dough will be quite stiff). Chill in a plastic bag for 30 minutes.

LIGHTLY DUST the work surface with flour and roll the pastry out to about 32 x 24 cm. Trim the edges, then cut the pastry into twelve 8 cm squares. Lightly oil the metal cannoli tubes. Wrap a pastry square diagonally around each tube, securing the overlapping corners with beaten egg and pressing them firmly together.

HEAT the oil in a deep-fat fryer or deep frying pan to about 180°C (350°F), or until a scrap of pastry dropped into the oil becomes crisp and golden, with a slightly blistered surface, in 15–20 seconds. If the oil starts to smoke it is too hot. Add the cannoli, a couple at a time, and deep-fry until golden and crisp. Remove with tongs and drain on paper towels. As soon as the tubes are cool enough to handle, slide them out and leave the pastries on a rack to cool.

TO MAKE the filling, mash the ricotta with a fork. Blend in the sugar and vanilla extract, then mix in the lemon zest, candied peel, glacé cherries and chocolate. Fill the pastries, either with a piping bag or a spoon. Arrange on a plate and dust with icing sugar for serving. The cannoli should be eaten soon after they are filled.

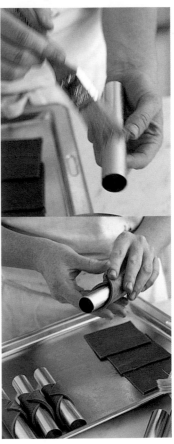

Traditional cannoli moulds need to be lightly greased before use. Wrap a pastry square around each tube, then deep-fry.

Almonds are native to the Mediterranean. In Italy fresh almonds are picked while they still have their green coating and the kernel is soft and a bit wet. They are then eaten on their own or served with cheese.

BISCOTTI

380 g plain flour
160 g caster sugar
3 eggs
1/2 teaspoon baking powder
1/2 teaspoon vanilla extract
150 g blanched almonds

MAKES 20

PREHEAT the oven to 180°C (350°F/Gas 4) and line two baking trays with baking parchment. Sieve the flour into a large bowl or food processor, add the sugar, eggs, baking powder, vanilla and a pinch of salt and mix or process until you have a smooth dough. Transfer to a floured surface and knead in the almonds.

DIVIDE the dough into two pieces and roll each one into a log about 20 cm long. Put on the baking trays and press down gently along the top to flatten the logs slightly. Bake for 25 minutes until the dough is gold in colour. Take the logs out of the oven and leave to cool slightly while you turn the oven down to 170°C (325°F/Gas 3).

CUT EACH log into 1 cm-thick diagonal slices, lay these back on the baking tray and return to the oven for 15 minutes until they start to brown and are dry to the touch. Store in an airtight container.

AMARETTI

125 g blanched almonds
125 g icing sugar
3 teaspoons plain flour
2 egg whites
75 g caster sugar
1 teaspoon almond extract

MAKES 15

PREHEAT the oven to 180°C (350°F/Gas 4). Put the almonds, icing sugar and flour in a pestle and mortar or food processor and grind to a fine powder (be careful not to overwork the mixture or it will become oily).

WHISK the egg whites in a clean dry glass bowl until soft peaks form. Add the caster sugar a tablespoon at a time and beat continuously until you have a stiff shiny mixture. Fold in the almond mixture and the almond extract until just blended.

SPOON the mixture into a piping bag with a 1 cm plain nozzle and pipe 3 cm-wide mounds, well spaced, onto a baking tray. Smooth the top of each biscuit with a damp finger and bake for 40 minutes until they are light brown. Turn off the oven, leave the door ajar and let the biscuits cool and dry out. Store in an airtight container.

SCHIACCIATA CON UVA

THIS BREAD IS A FLORENTINE SPECIALITY, TRADITIONALLY MADE IN TUSCANY DURING THE GRAPE HARVEST. THE RAISINS, REPRESENTING LAST SEASON'S GRAPES, ARE COMBINED WITH THE NEW SEASON'S GRAPES TAKEN FROM THE PRESENT HARVEST.

100 g raisins
90 ml sweet Marsala
150 ml milk
2 teaspoons dried yeast or
    15 g fresh yeast
125 g caster sugar
300 g plain flour
olive oil
500 g black seedless grapes

SERVES 6

PUT the raisins and Marsala in a bowl to soak. Warm the milk to hand hot and place in a small bowl. Stir in the yeast and 1 teaspoon of the sugar and set aside in a draught-free spot. If the yeast does not bubble and foam in 5 minutes, throw it away and try again.

PUT the flour, 90 g of the sugar and a pinch of salt in a bowl and mix together. Add the yeast mixture and mix until the dough starts to come together in a clump. Transfer to a lightly floured surface and knead for 6–8 minutes. Add a little more flour or a few drops of warm water if necessary to give a soft, but not sticky, dough.

RUB the inside of a large bowl with olive oil. Roll the ball of dough around in the bowl to coat it with oil, then cut a cross on the top of the ball with a sharp knife. Leave the dough in the bowl, cover with a tea towel or put in a plastic bag and leave in a draught-free spot for 1–1½ hours until doubled in size.

DRAIN the raisins and squeeze them dry. Lightly dust a baking tray with flour. Punch down the dough (give it one good blow in the centre with your fist to expel the air) and divide in two. Shape each portion into a disc about 20 cm in diameter and place one disc on the tray. Scatter half the grapes and half the raisins on top, then cover with the second disc of dough. Scatter the remaining grapes and raisins over the top. Cover again and leave for 1 hour to rise again and double in size.

PREHEAT the oven to 180°C (350°F/Gas 4). Sprinkle the surface of the bread with the remaining sugar. Bake for 40–50 minutes, or until golden.

Pile the grapes and raisins into the centre of the base, so that when the top goes on they are almost covered and stay soft when they are cooking. Scatter the raisins and grapes on top and press them into the dough so they don't burn as they cook.

PANFORTE

PANFORTE MEANS 'STRONG BREAD', AN APT DESCRIPTION FOR THIS DENSE, FRUITY LOAF THAT STILL RETAINS ITS MEDIEVAL FLAVOUR. PANFORTE IS ALSO KNOWN AS SIENA CAKE—SIENA POSSIBLY BEING THE FIRST ITALIAN CITY TO USE SUGAR AND SPICES SUCH AS WHITE PEPPER.

110 g hazelnuts
110 g almonds
125 g candied mixed peel, chopped
100 g candied pineapple, chopped
grated zest of 1 lemon
75 g plain flour
1 teaspoon ground cinnamon
1/4 teaspoon ground coriander
1/4 teaspoon ground cloves
1/4 teaspoon grated nutmeg
pinch of white pepper
150 g sugar
4 tablespoons honey
50 g unsalted butter
icing sugar

MAKES ONE 23 CM CAKE

LINE a 23 cm springform tin with rice paper or baking parchment and grease well with butter. Toast the nuts under a hot grill, turning them so they brown on all sides, then leave to cool. Put the nuts in a bowl with the mixed peel, pineapple, lemon zest, flour and spices and toss together. Preheat the oven to 150°C (300°F/Gas 2).

PUT the sugar, honey and butter in a saucepan and melt them together. Cook the syrup until it reaches 120°C on a sugar thermometer, or a little of it dropped into cold water forms a soft ball when moulded between your finger and thumb.

POUR the syrup into the nut mixture and mix well, working fast before it stiffens too much. Pour straight into the tin, smooth the surface and bake for 35 minutes. (Unlike other cakes this will neither firm up as it cooks or colour at all so you need to time it carefully.)

COOL IN the tin until the cake firms up enough to remove the side of the tin. Peel off the paper and leave to cool completely. Dust the top heavily with icing sugar.

The hills around Siena.

POLENTA CAKE

IN THE MOUNTAINOUS REGIONS OF NORTH ITALY POLENTA WAS TRADITIONALLY THE STAPLE DIET OF THE POOR. TODAY IT IS HAVING A RESURGENCE OF POPULARITY. COARSE- OR FINE-GRAINED POLENTA WILL GIVE THIS CAKE DIFFERENT TEXTURES, BUT EITHER IS FINE. ENJOY WITH A GLASS OF VIN SANTO.

45 g sultanas
2 tablespoons brandy
225 g ricotta
250 g caster sugar
225 g polenta
pinch of grated nutmeg
1/2 teaspoon grated lemon zest
1/4 teaspoon vanilla extract
20 g unsalted butter, chilled and cut
    into small cubes
2 tablespoons pine nuts
icing sugar

MAKES ONE 25 CM CAKE

PUT the sultanas and brandy in a small bowl with enough water to cover them and leave for 30 minutes. Drain and dry well on paper towels.

PREHEAT the oven to 160°C (315°F/Gas 2–3) and grease a 25 cm loose-bottomed or spring-form cake tin with a tight-fitting base.

PUT the ricotta in a large bowl and add 450 ml cold water. Beat with a wire whisk or electric beaters until smooth. Don't be alarmed by the thinness of the mixture—it can be very liquid, depending on the brand of ricotta used. Add the sugar and beat until smooth, then stir in the polenta, nutmeg, lemon zest, vanilla and sultanas.

POUR the mixture into the tin. Dot the surface with butter and sprinkle the pine nuts on top. Put the tin on a baking tray to catch any drips and bake for about 1 1/2 hours until golden and set. Serve warm or cold, dusted with icing sugar and accompanied by whipped cream.

Sprinkling the polenta in from a height distributes it evenly and makes it easier to whisk in. Tip the mixture into the tin so that the sultanas are spread evenly. Dotting the top of the cake with butter gives it a golden finish.

HAZELNUT AND CHOCOLATE CAKE

140 g skinned hazelnuts
3 tablespoons cocoa powder
60 g plain flour
30 g self-raising flour
185 g soft brown sugar
250 g unsalted butter, softened
4 eggs, separated
icing sugar

SERVES 8

TOAST the hazelnuts under a hot grill, turning them so they brown on all sides. Leave them to cool, then put in a food processor and process until fine (don't overprocess or they will become oily), or chop finely with a knife. Transfer to a bowl with the cocoa powder and sifted flours. Preheat the oven to 180°C (350°F/Gas 4).

BEAT TOGETHER the sugar and butter until very creamy. Add the egg yolks one at a time, mixing well after each addition. Add the hazelnut mixture and stir well. Whisk the egg whites in a clean dry glass bowl until stiff peaks form, then fold into the mixture. Pour into the tin and bake for 50 minutes or until a skewer inserted into the centre comes out clean. Rest for 15 minutes, then cool on a wire rack. Dust with icing sugar before serving.

In Tuscany chestnuts are grown in quantity. The season is short—early November until Christmas—so they are also dried for year-round use. The dried chestnuts are soaked in water, then boiled in milk for soups or sweet desserts.

CHESTNUT CAKE

400 g chestnuts or 250 g cooked
   peeled chestnuts
5 egg yolks
200 g caster sugar
100 g unsalted butter, softened
1 tablespoon grated lemon zest
150 g ground almonds
2 tablespoons plain flour
4 egg whites

SERVES 8

PREHEAT the oven to 180°C (350°F/Gas 4) and grease and flour a 20 cm cake tin.

BOIL the chestnuts in a saucepan of water for 25 minutes, or until they are tender. Drain, peel and, while still hot, purée and sieve. (If you are using the cooked chestnuts, simply purée them.)

WHISK the egg yolks and sugar until light and fluffy. Add the butter, lemon zest, chestnut purée, ground almonds and flour and stir well. Whisk the egg whites until soft peaks form and fold into the mixture. Pour into the tin and bake for 50–60 minutes. Cool on a wire rack and serve with whipped cream.

CHESTNUT CAKE

VENETIAN RICE PUDDING

625 ml milk
250 ml double cream
1 vanilla pod, split
50 g caster sugar
1/4 teaspoon ground cinnamon
pinch of grated nutmeg
1 tablespoon grated orange zest
75 g sultanas
2 tablespoons brandy or sweet
  Marsala
100 g arborio or vialone nano rice

SERVES 4

PUT the milk, cream and vanilla pod in a heavy-based saucepan and bring just to the boil, then remove from the heat. Add the sugar, cinnamon, nutmeg and orange zest and set aside.

PUT the sultanas and brandy in a small bowl and leave to soak. Add the rice to the infused milk and return to the heat. Bring to a simmer and stir slowly for about 35 minutes, or until the rice is creamy. Stir in the sultanas and remove the vanilla pod at the end. Serve warm or cold.

Rice grown in Italy is much more absorbent than that grown elsewhere. It is ideal for risotto, and also for rice-based desserts.

BAKED FIGS

WHEN NOT IN ITALY, YOU'LL HAVE TO BUY CANTUCCI AT SPECIALIST ITALIAN GROCERS, ALTHOUGH SOME LARGER SUPERMARKETS DO STOCK THEM. DON'T WASTE THE REST OF THE PACKET—SERVE THEM AFTER THE FIGS, FOR DIPPING IN AFTER-DINNER DRINKS LIKE VIN SANTO OR ESPRESSO.

3 cantucci (biscotti di Prato)
1 teaspoon grated lemon zest
60 ml double cream
4 purple figs, ripe but firm
juice of 1/2 lemon
1 tablespoon brown sugar

SERVES 4

PREHEAT the oven to 210°C (415°F/Gas 6–7) and lightly grease a shallow ovenproof dish large enough to hold eight fig halves, overlapping slightly. Crush the cantucci with a heavy rolling pin. Combine the crumbs with half the lemon zest and half the cream.

SLICE EACH fig in half lengthways and drizzle the lemon juice over the cut surfaces. Fill the figs with the cantucci filling, pressing it loosely onto the centres of the cut surfaces. Arrange the figs in the dish, with each stem end slightly overlapping the base of the fig in front. Pour the remaining cream over the top and sprinkle with the remaining lemon zest, then the sugar.

BAKE FOR 10 minutes or until the sugar melts and a little syrup forms in the dish. Serve warm with a little of the syrup spooned on top, with mascarpone or whipped cream and the rest of the packet of cantucci.

BAKED FIGS

BASICS

Pasta is traditionally made on the work surface and not in a bowl. Roll it by hand or with a pasta machine—whichever method you choose, it must be thin enough to read a newspaper through.

PASTA

500 g 00 (doppio zero) or plain flour
4 eggs
chilled water

MAKES 700 G

MOUND the flour on a work surface or in a large bowl. Make a well in the centre. Break the eggs into the well and whisk with a fork, incorporating the flour as you whisk. You may need to add a little chilled water (1/4 teaspoon at a time) to make a loosely massed dough. Turn the dough onto a lightly floured surface—it should be soft, pliable and dry to the touch. Knead for 6–8 minutes, or until smooth and elastic with a slightly glossy appearance. Cover with a tea towel and leave for 30 minutes. The dough is then ready to roll out.

TO MAKE the dough in a processor, mix the flour for 2–3 seconds, then add the eggs with the motor running. Mix again for 5 seconds, or until the mixture looks like coarse meal. Mix until a loose ball forms, then continue for 4–5 seconds until the machine slows and stops. If the dough seems too sticky to form a smooth ball, add 2 teaspoons flour, mix briefly and continue adding small amounts of flour until the ball forms. If the mixture is too dry, add chilled water, a teaspoon at a time. Transfer to a lightly floured surface and knead for 2–3 minutes until smooth and elastic. Cover with a tea towel and leave for 30 minutes.

TO ROLL OUT the dough, divide into two or three manageable portions. Work with one portion at a time, keeping the rest covered. Flatten the dough onto a lightly floured surface and roll out from the centre to the outer edge, rotating the dough often. When you have a 5 mm thick circle of dough, fold it in half and roll it out again. Do this eight times to give a smooth circle of pasta, then roll to a thickness of 2.5 mm (mend any tears with a little pasta from the outside of the circle and a little water). Transfer to a lightly floured tea towel. If the pasta is to be filled, keep it covered and don't allow it to dry out. If the sheets are to be cut into lengths or shapes, leave them uncovered while you roll out the other portions, so that the surface moisture will dry slightly before cutting.

IF YOU have a pasta machine, work the dough through the rollers, making the setting smaller each time until the dough is the correct thickness.

PIZZA DOUGH

1 tablespoon caster sugar
2 teaspoons dried yeast or
  15 g fresh yeast
215 ml lukewarm water
450 g plain flour
1/2 teaspoon salt
3 tablespoons olive oil
cornmeal

MAKES TWO 30 CM
PIZZA BASES

PUT the sugar and yeast in a small bowl and stir in 90 ml of the water. Leave in a draught-free spot to activate. If the yeast does not bubble and foam in 5 minutes, throw it away and start again.

MIX the flour and salt in a bowl or in a food processor fitted with a plastic blade. Add the olive oil, remaining water and the yeast mixture. Mix until the dough loosely clumps together. Transfer to a lightly floured surface and knead for 8 minutes, adding a little flour or a few drops of warm water if necessary, until you have a soft dough that is not sticky but is dry to the touch.

RUB the inside of a large bowl with olive oil. Roll the ball of dough around in the bowl to coat it with oil, then cut a shallow cross on the top of the ball with a sharp knife. Leave the dough in the bowl, cover with a tea towel or put in a plastic bag and leave in a draught-free spot for 1–1 1/2 hours until doubled in size (or leave in the fridge for 8 hours to rise slowly).

PUNCH DOWN the dough to its original size, then divide into two portions. (At this stage the dough can be stored in the fridge for up to 4 hours, or frozen. Bring back to room temperature before continuing.)

WORKING with one portion at a time, push the dough out to make a thick circle. Use the heels of your hands and work from the centre of the circle outwards, to flatten the dough into a 30 cm circle with a slightly raised rim. (If you find it difficult to push the dough out by hand you can use a rolling pin.) The pizza dough is now ready to use, as instructed in the recipe. Cook on a lightly oiled tray, dusted with cornmeal, and get it into the oven as quickly as possible.

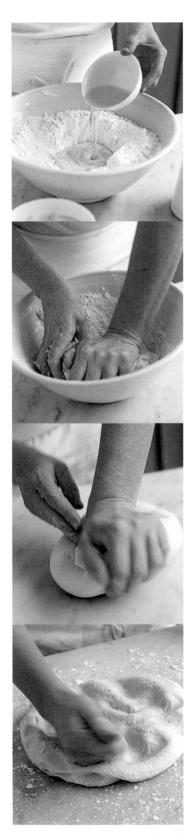

Knead the dough by stretching it away from you and then folding it back on itself. Use your fist to squash it into a flat circle. You will need to push quite hard.

Make the dough in a large bowl so you have enough room to bring it together. Knead on a well-floured surface until the dough is really elastic. Use the heel of your hand to stretch it into a rectangle.

FOCACCIA DOUGH

$1/2$ teaspoon caster sugar
2 teaspoons dried yeast or
   15 g fresh yeast
800 ml lukewarm water
1 kg plain flour
2 teaspoons salt
2 tablespoons olive oil
cornmeal

MAKES 2 FOCACCIA

PUT the sugar and yeast in a small bowl and stir in 60 ml of the water. Leave in a draught-free spot to activate. If the yeast does not bubble and foam in 5 minutes, throw it away and start again.

MIX the flour and salt in a bowl or in a food processor fitted with a plastic blade. Add the olive oil, the yeast mixture and three-quarters of the remaining water. Mix, then add the rest of the water, a little at a time, until the dough loosely clumps together. Transfer to a lightly floured surface and knead for 8 minutes until smooth, or until the impression made by a finger springs back immediately.

RUB the inside of a large bowl with olive oil. Roll the ball of dough around in the bowl to coat it with oil, then cut a shallow cross on the top of the ball with a sharp knife. Leave the dough in the bowl, cover with a tea towel or put in a plastic bag and leave in a draught-free spot for $1–1^{1}/2$ hours until doubled in size (or leave in the fridge for 8 hours to rise slowly).

PUNCH DOWN the dough to its original size, then divide into two portions. (At this stage the dough can be stored in the fridge for 4 hours, or frozen. Bring back to room temperature before continuing.) Roll each portion of dough out to a 28 x 20 cm rectangle, then use the heels of your hands, working from the centre of the dough outwards, to make a 38 x 28 cm rectangle.

LIGHTLY OIL 2 baking trays and dust with cornmeal. Put a portion of dough in the centre of each tray and press out to fill the tray. Slide the trays inside a plastic bag. Seal and leave in a draught-free spot for 2 hours to rise again. The focaccia dough is now ready to use, as instructed in the recipe.

BECHAMEL SAUCE

65 g butter
40 g plain flour
pinch of grated nutmeg
600 ml milk
1 bay leaf

MAKES 800 ML

HEAT the butter in a saucepan over low heat. Add the flour and nutmeg and cook, stirring, for 1 minute. Remove from the heat and gradually stir in the milk. Add the bay leaf, return to the heat and simmer, stirring often, until the sauce thickens. Season, cover with clingfilm to prevent a skin forming, and cool. Discard the bay leaf.

BECHAMEL SAUCE

TOMATO SAUCE

120 g plum tomatoes
3 basil leaves
2 garlic cloves, crushed
1 tablespoon tomato passata
2 teaspoons extra virgin olive oil

MAKES 200 ML

CORE the tomatoes and purée in a food processor with the basil leaves (or chop the tomatoes and basil very finely and stir together). Stir in the garlic, passata and olive oil and season well. Leave for at least 30 minutes before serving to allow the flavours to blend. Use on pizzas, toss through pasta or serve with arancini or suppli.

TOMATO SAUCE

PESTO

2 garlic cloves
50 g pine nuts
80 g basil leaves
4 tablespoons grated Parmesan
150 ml extra virgin olive oil

MAKES 200 ML

PUT the garlic, pine nuts, basil and Parmesan in a mortar and pestle or a food processor and pound or mix to a paste. Add the oil in a steady stream, mixing continuously. Add salt if necessary. Refrigerate in a sterilized jar, covered with a layer of olive oil, for up to 3 weeks.

SALSA VERDE

1¹/₂ tablespoons fresh white
  breadcrumbs
1 tablespoon milk
1 hard-boiled egg yolk
2 anchovy fillets
1 tablespoon capers
5 tablespoons finely chopped
  parsley, mint and basil
1 garlic clove, crushed
75 ml extra virgin olive oil

MAKES 200 ML

SOAK the breadcrumbs in the milk for 10 minutes. Finely chop together the egg yolk, anchovy and capers. Add the herbs, garlic and soaked breadcrumbs and mix with a fork. Slowly blend in the olive oil until the sauce is smooth and thick. Season with pepper, then set aside for at least 1 hour before using.

SALSA VERDE

VINAIGRETTE

2 tablespoons lemon juice
4 tablespoons olive oil
2 teaspoons finely chopped onion
   or 1 finely chopped shallot
1 tablespoon chopped parsley

MAKES 180 ML

MAKE the dressing by combining all the ingredients. Season with salt and pepper.

OVEN-DRIED TOMATOES

OVEN-DRIED TOMATOES

24 plum tomatoes
sea salt
4 garlic cloves, crushed
1/2 tablespoon extra virgin olive oil
24 basil leaves
1 mild red chilli, cut into 24 small
   pieces
1/2 tablespoon dried oregano
750 ml olive oil

FILLS A 2 LITRE JAR

PREHEAT the oven to 75°C (150°F/Gas 1/4). Core each tomato and slice almost in half along its length, with just the skin keeping it together. Open out butterfly-fashion and space out, cut side up, on wire racks. Sprinkle with sea salt and bake for about 8 hours, until dark and almost leathery, but not crisp. Cool and store in sterilized jars for up to six months, or preserve as below.

MIX the garlic with the extra virgin olive oil. Brush one half of each tomato, then place a basil leaf, piece of chilli and sprinkling of oregano on top. Fold the other half over to enclose and place in a sterilized jar. Pour in the olive oil to cover the tomatoes and push down firmly to expel any air. Seal and refrigerate for up to two months.

GIARDINIERA

GIARDINIERA (GARDEN PICKLES)

280 g carrots, cut into short lengths
280 g pearl onions
220 g small fresh gherkins
875 ml white wine vinegar
1 tablespoon sea salt
2 tablespoons honey
220 g stringless green beans, cut
   into short lengths
10 black peppercorns
6 whole cloves
5 juniper berries
2 bay leaves

FILLS A 1.25 LITRE JAR

PREHEAT the oven to 120°C (250°F/Gas 1/2). Put the carrot, onions, gherkins, vinegar, salt and honey in a saucepan with 600 ml water and bring to the boil. Reduce the heat and simmer for 20 minutes. Add the beans and simmer for 5 minutes, or until the vegetables are tender but still slightly crisp.

DRAIN the vegetables, reserving the liquid. Arrange the vegetables in a sterilized 1.25 litre jar and add the peppercorns, cloves, juniper berries and bay leaves. Pour in the liquid to cover the vegetables. Seal and refrigerate for 24 hours before use. Will keep for up to two months.

IN TUSCANY, one of Italy's most famous wine-producing areas, you can see both the most traditional and the most innovative of Italian wine-making today. Agricola San Felice is a 220-hectare vineyard situated in the prestigious Chianti Classico area, where many of the vineyards proudly display a black rooster on their bottles—a sign that they are members of the Chianti Classico Consortium. The DOC regulations

WINE

THE HISTORY OF WINE IN ITALY STRETCHES BACK THOUSANDS OF YEARS. THE ETRUSCANS MAY WELL HAVE ENJOYED WINE, THOUGH IT WAS THE GREEKS AND LATER THE ROMANS WHO SAW THE REAL POTENTIAL IN ITALY FOR CULTIVATING VINES.

A terrain that ranges from the Alps to the sunbaked south and a Mediterranean climate create a perfect environment for producing a huge variety of unique wines. While today's wines are very different from the rich, aged wines enjoyed by the Romans, there can still be found some continuation in wine-making methods and traditions, particularly in some of Italy's most classic wines—Recioto and Amarone della Valpolicella and Vin Santo, where grapes are dried out

before pressing. While traditional methods are respected and preserved, and many Italian wine producers still consist of a family working their own vineyards, the Italians have also been quick to modernize their cellars and innovative in producing new wines. French varieties have been planted alongside Italian varieties and new technology installed.

DENOMINAZIONE DI ORIGINE CONTROLLATA
Italy's reputation worldwide for its wines was initially based on easy-drinking bottles of Soave, Frascati, Lambrusco, Asti-Spumante and particularly the distinctive bottles of Chianti, which graced trattorias all over the world. While these wines were popular and profitable, the quality was variable and in 1963, the Italian government introduced laws called the *denominazione di origine controllata (DOC)* to control wine production. This has led to a rise in standards and Italy's place as one of the world's leading wine exporters. In Italy, wine is an important part of every meal and is seen as a partner for food, rather than a drink to be drunk on its own.

AS WELL AS producing traditional Chianti Classico, San Felice has long been involved in viticultural research, most notably with its *Vitiarium,* a two-hectare vineyard where about 300 less well-known Tuscan vines are being cultivated. It was this innovative approach to wine-making that led to *Vigorello,* a precursor to today's super-Tuscans, first being produced here in 1968. The super-Tuscans are inspired by the great wines of

introduced for Chianti in 1967 froze in time what was already a disputed 'recipe' for that wine, allowing up to 30 per cent white grapes to be added to the red Sangiovese grapes. Later DOCG regulations improved on this situation until, by 1996, Chianti could be made with very few, or even no, white grapes. Today San Felice produces some very high-quality Chianti Classico wines, including *Il Grigio, a* Chianti Classico Riserva.

BUYING ITALIAN WINE

Good wines are produced in every one of Italy's regions. Even in the hot South, some excellent wines can be found, while Piemonte and Tuscany produce red wines of international repute. When buying Italian wines, the DOC label guarantees authenticity and certain minimum standards of quality. Some of the country's finest wines, such as Barolo, Barbaresco, Chianti and Brunello di Montalcino are controlled under the much stricter *denominazione di origine controllata e garantita* (DOCG) regulations, and these wines are often of a very high quality. However, some of Italy's wine makers choose to produce wines that do not conform to the regulations required to obtain DOC status, particularly those regarding grape varieties. There are now attempts to classify these 'super-table' wines, many rating among Italy's finest, under a new IGT (*Indicazione Geographica Tipica*) system, but many are still sold as just *vino da tavola*. In Italy, an *Enoteca* is a 'wine library'—a specialist wine shop that can give advice on buying wines.

ORDERING ITALIAN WINE

In many restaurants in Italy, you may not even be passed a wine list. Instead, the choice is between the house red or white wine. If there is a wine list, you may still choose to pick a local wine, many of which are made to be the perfect partner for the food of their region.

READING ITALIAN LABELS

ABBOCCATO medium dry
AMABILE medium sweet
AMARONE dry (literally bitter)
CLASSICO wines that come from the best part of a DOC area
DOLCE sweet
FRIZZANTE slightly tizzy, usually naturally fizzy from fermentation
RECIOTO wine made from selected (ie riper) bunches of grapes
RISERVA wine that has undergone a longer period of ageing
SECCO dry
SPUMANTE fully sparkling
SUPERIORE higher degree of alcohol than normal

Bordeaux and choose to exist outside the DOC regulations. Marketed often to international acclaim, they are sold under the humble *vino da tavola* status. Vigorello ia made from 70 per cent Sangiovese mixed with 30 per cent of the foreign Cabernet Sauvignon. The grapes are fermented in stainless-steel tanks, then the wine aged for 18 months in French oak barriques in San Felice's cellars to give a smooth finish to the wine.

GLOSSARY OF ITALIAN FOOD AND COOKING

al dente Meaning 'to the tooth'. Pasta and risotto rice are cooked until they are *al dente*—the outside is tender but the centre still has a little resistance or 'bite'. Pasta cooked beyond this point becomes soggy.

amaretti Small biscuits like macaroons, made from sweet and bitter almonds. They vary in size, but are usually 2–3 cm wide.

artichoke (*carciofo*) The edible flower of a member of the thistle family. Some have thorns and the types vary greatly in size. The largest are usually boiled, but the smallest and most tender can be eaten raw as antipasto. Most common varieties include Romanesco (large and purple), Precoce di Chioggia (large and green), Violetto Toscano (small and tender enough to eat raw) and Spinoso di Palermo (a purple variety from Sicily).

bocconcini Means literally 'small mouthful' and is used to describe various foods, but generally refers to small balls of mozzarella, about the size of walnuts.

bouquet garni A bundle of herbs used to flavour dishes. Made by tying sprigs of parsley, thyme, celery leaves and a bay leaf in either a piece of muslin or portion of leek.

bresaola Lean beef that is cured and air-dried for 2–3 months—a speciality of the Valtellina Valley in Lombardia. Has a dark red colour and stronger flavour than prosciutto. Serve thinly sliced.

cantucci Tuscan almond biscuits, also known as *biscotti di Prato*. These hard, double-baked biscuits often contain whole almonds. They are usually eaten dipped into a dessert wine such as vin santo.

caperberries The fruit of the caper bush, which appear after the flowers. They are usually preserved in brine and served as an accompaniment, like olives.

capers The pickled flowers of the caper bush. These are available preserved in brine, vinegar or salt and should be rinsed well and squeezed dry before use.

cardoons Similar to the artichoke plant, cardoons have large leaves and long stems. Unlike artichokes, it is the stems that are eaten rather than the flowers. The stalks are usually blanched like celery.

casalinga Means 'home-made' or 'homely'. When attributed to sausages or salami, it generally means having a coarse texture and earthy flavour.

cavolo nero Cabbage with long leaves that are so dark green they appear to be almost black. Used mainly in Tuscan cooking. If unavailable, Savoy cabbage can be used.

cetriolini Small gherkins. If unavailable, use cornichons or small cocktail gherkins.

ciabatta Slipper-shaped Italian bread with a rough, open texture. They are made from a very wet dough, which allows large bubbles to form and gives a thin crust. Ciabatta quickly goes stale and is best eaten on the day it is bought or made.

cipolline Small white onions, usually flattened in appearance rather than round.

coppa A type of cured pork made from half pork fat and half pig's neck and shoulder. It is rolled and cured in a casing and, when sliced, resembles a fatty sausage.

cotechino A sausage made from pork and pork rind, giving it a gelatinous texture. Cotechino is flavoured with cloves and cinnamon and needs to be cooked before eating.

country-style bread Any bread that is bought as a whole loaf and has a rough texture. Pugliese, ciabatta and pane Toscano are all examples. Other white bread is not a suitable substitute.

croccante Caramelized nuts, usually almonds but sometimes hazelnuts (these are also known as pralines).

doppio zero (00) flour The finest grade of flour, made from soft wheat (*grano tenero*) and mainly used for making cakes and fresh egg pasta.

farro A type of spelt grain, farro is used in soups and stews in a similar way to barley. If farro is unavailable, spelt or barley can be used. Farro is most commonly used in the cuisines of the areas where it is grown—Tuscany, Umbria and Lazio.

finocchiona A type of salami from Tuscany, flavoured with wild fennel seeds. The salami is very often large and is aged for up to a year before use. It also comes in a more crumbly version called sbriciolona.

flat-leaf parsley Also known as Italian or continental parsley. Used as an ingredient rather than a garnish, unlike curly parsley.

fontina A traditional mountain cheese from the Valle d'Aosta in Piemonte. Full-fat and semi-soft with a sweetish flavour, fontina melts evenly and well and so is particularly good for cooking.

Gorgonzola A blue cheese, originally made in Gorgonzola in Lombardia but now produced in other regions as well. It melts well and is often used in sauces. If not available, use another full-fat blue cheese.

juniper berries Blackish-purple berries with a resin flavour. Used in stews and game dishes. Crush the berries slightly before use to release their flavour.

Marsala A fortified wine from Marsala in Sicily that comes in varying degrees of dryness and sweetness. Dry Marsalas are used in savoury dishes, and sweet ones in desserts such as zabaione. Do not try to use sweet Marsala in savoury dishes.

mascarpone A cream cheese originally from Lombardia. Made with cream rather than milk, it is very high in fat. Mascarpone is generally used in desserts such as tiramisu or instead of cream in sauces.

misticanza A Roman salad that was once made of wild greens. Today it is generally a mixture of rocket, purslane, sorrel, mint, dandelion, wild fennel and endive with some lettuce. In Umbria it also refers to a mixture of dried beans used for soups.

mortadella A large, finely textured pork sausage, with lengths of lard running through it. Some versions contain pistachio nuts and all should be eaten thinly sliced or in cubes and very fresh. Traditionally made in Bologna, the sausage is also known as bologna or boloney in the USA.

olive Eating olives can be named after where they come from, such as Ligurian; their curing style, such as Sicilian; or their variety, such as Cerignola. Though green and black olives have a different flavour, they can be used interchangeably in recipes unless the final colour is a factor.

olive oil Extra-virgin and virgin olive oils are pressed without any heat or chemicals and are best used in simple uncooked dishes and for salads. Pure olive oil can be used for cooking or deep-frying. Different varieties of olives are grown all over Italy and the oil of each region has a distinctive taste. Tuscan oil tends to be full-bodied and peppery; Ligurian oil pale and subtle; and Pugliese and Sicilian oil fruity and sharp.

pancetta Cured belly of pork, somewhat like streaky bacon. Available in flat pieces or rolled up (arrotolata), and both smoked and unsmoked. Generally used, either sliced or cut into cubes, as an ingredient in dishes like spaghetti carbonara.

Parma ham This prosciutto comes from traditionally reared pigs fed on the whey from making Parmigiano Reggiano. It has a sweet taste and is only flavoured with salt. Parma hams can be identified by the stamp on the skin showing the five-pointed star of the Dukes of Parma. Other prosciutto can be used if Parma ham is unavailable.

passata Meaning 'puréed', this most commonly refers to a smooth uncooked tomato pulp bought in tins or jars. Best without added herbs and flavourings.

pecorino One of Italy's most popular cheeses, virtually every region produces a version. Made from sheep's milk and always by the same method, although the result varies according to the milk and ageing process used. Pecorino Romano is a well-known hard variety from Lazio and Sardinia.

peperoncini The Italian name for chillies, these are popular in the cooking of the South, and are also served there as a condiment. The smallest are called diavolilli.

polenta The name of the dish and also the ingredient itself, which is ground corn. The cornmeal comes in different grades of coarseness. Finer varieties are better in cakes and coarse ones to accompany stews. A white cornmeal is also available.

porcini The Italian name for a cep or boletus mushroom. Usually bought dried and reconstituted in boiling water, but available fresh in the spring and autumn.

prosciutto Italian name for ham. Prosciutto crudo is cured ham and includes Parma ham and San Daniele. Prosciutto cotto is cooked ham.

provolone Curd cheese made from cows' milk. The curds are spun and worked into large pear- or tube-shaped cheeses, then immersed in brine and bound with string. Available fresh or matured and eaten as a table cheese or used in cooking.

radicchio A salad leaf of the chicory family with slightly bitter red leaves. There are several varieties: radicchio di Castelfranco, di Chioggia and rosso di Verona are similar to a red cabbage with round leaves; radicchio di Treviso has longer, pointed leaves.

risotto rice Round-grained, very absorbent rice, cultivated in northern Italy. Risotto rice comes in four categories, classified not by quality but by the size of each grain. The smallest, Riso Comune (common rice) is very quick to cook (12–13 minutes), and is ideal for rice pudding. Semifino rice includes varieties like vialone nano and cooks in about 15 minutes. Fino takes a minute longer and has more bite. The largest, Superfino, includes arborio and carnaroli and takes about 20 minutes.

soffritto The flavour base for many soups, stews and risottos. Soffritto is a mixture of fried ingredients like onion, celery, carrot, garlic, pancetta and herbs. It means literally to 'under-fry' and the mixture should be sweated rather than coloured.

squid/cuttlefish ink Used to colour and flavour pasta and risotto. The ink is stored in a sac that can be removed from whole squid and cuttlefish or bought in sachets from fishmongers or delicatessens.

Taleggio A mountain cheese originally from the Italian Alps near Bergamo, but now also made in other regions. Taleggio is a very good table and cooking cheese and should be eaten young—its flavour becomes more acidic with age. It is made in squares and has a pink-yellow crust and creamy centre.

truffles Both black and white truffles can be found in Italy. The black ones come from Umbria (especially around Norcia), Piemonte and Emilia-Romagna. The white ones come from Alba (considered the best), Emilia-Romagna, Le Marche, Tuscany and Umbria. Fresh truffles are very expensive but only a tiny amount is needed. Preserved truffles are also available, as is truffle oil.

vin santo A golden dessert wine eaten with cantucci biscuits. Now made all over Italy, but the best known is made in Tuscany.

zucchini The Italian name for courgettes.

INDEX